Herman C. Dorner

Guide to the New York Aquarium

Herman C. Dorner

Guide to the New York Aquarium

ISBN/EAN: 9783337270087

Printed in Europe, USA, Canada, Australia, Japan

Cover: Foto ©Andreas Hilbeck / pixelio.de

More available books at **www.hansebooks.com**

GUIDE

TO THE

NEW YORK AQUARIUM

BY THE MANAGER,
H. DORNER, Ph.D.
Late of the Hamburg Zoological Garden and Aquarium.

CHAS. REICHE & BRO.,
PROPRIETORS.

NEW YORK:
ATHENEUM PUBLISHING HOUSE,
D. I. CARSON & CO.,
100 NASSAU STREET.

INTRODUCTION.

Now that we have a New York Aquarium where we can go and lounge and study Icthyology, as Mirabeau wished to die "to the sound of delicious music," we appreciate what a boon it is, and we have a glimmering idea that it is an absolute necessity. All successful affairs are necessities; it is only the black list of failures that shows how many superfluities designing capitalists have endeavored to thrust upon society. But no one, perhaps, in looking at the preserved Octopus, or in watching the rainbow hues of the gold fish tank would imagine what a terribly arduous undertaking it was, this giving to New

York an institution of instruction and recreation such as she needed. When Mr. W. C. COUP and CHAS. REICHE & BROTHER first conceived the idea of the Aquarium and came to the point when they decided to build it, they knew that a mammoth task was before them. As the work progressed, the difficulties encountered convinced them that they were not mistaken. These difficulties were as numerous as they were unexpected, and it may truthfully be said, that the construction of so peculiar an edifice was, in a measure, groping one's way through experimental fog with the lantern of science. One day it would be that, owing to defective glass, the tanks would burst and flood the building with water. Then the fish would meet with accidents and die. In one clock beat the beautiful results of a two months' voyage in tropical seas has been rendered useless. Notwithstanding all these discouragements they persevered, tying up the thread where it broke, and patiently going on, backing their faith with their tank accounts, until the present handsome structure, and the marvellous collection of fishes and animals are the combined results. They may well be proud of the work that has cost them so much thought and money. So much more capital than that originally calculated upon was required for the completion of the gigantic undertaking, and for the proper equipment of the edifice, that Mr. W. C. COUP resolved to associate with himself in its active management the two liberal-hearted gentlemen, Messrs. CHAS. and HENRY REICHE, and from that day, with the additional added capital and facilities, the enterprise went ahead as if by magic, and the establishment was finally formally thrown open to the public on October 10th, 1876. In the association of the Messrs. REICHE, the enterprise seemed to obtain all that was required. They brought the facilities of their vast business, the years of knowledge and the great experience gained in collecting animals and curiosities from all parts of the world. To these gentlemen is due the credit of first bringing to this country the beautiful and gorgeous fishes of Japan and China, the marine animals and fishes of Europe, and the rare creatures of Central Africa. Their army of collectors, resident in all parts of the world, constantly on the lookout for that which is strange or rare in nature, were and are controlled by the head—Mr. Henry Reiche—residing in this city. To these collectors were given orders that Aquarium objects should be captured and transported here together with other curiosities, and in obedience to these instructions the recesses of almost wholly unexplored regions of uncivilized countries were successfully searched and their treasures laid at the door of our citizens, and where they are in such countless numbers, that, as the venerable poet, William Cullen Bryant, said in a published letter to the New York Journals, "we have an institution where one can learn more in two hours than from weeks of study." Not long after the brilliant prospects of the establishment were again clouded by misfortune and accident, the wholesale loss of costly whales and fishes. The same spirit of indomitable pluck was manifested again, and in a very short space of time the southern seas were white with Aquarium fleets in quest of new curiosities. The liberality and daring enterprise of the management have brought about their legitimate results—New York has now a resort that ranks among her foremost attractions. It is a delight for him who wishes merely to be entertained; it is an invaluable college for the student of fishes and the lover of aquaria. There is a growing taste in society for this latter branch of household adornment, and although text-books are valuable aids, there is nothing like the reality, in all its technical beauty, for the enthusiastic. As a recent article upon the subject says: "A well regulated aquarium is indeed a beautiful ornament for the home, and one which is a perpetual source of amusement and instruction. It has the peculiar advantage of making us acquainted with forms and habits of animated existence, which are commonly hid from our inspection. Thus its influence upon the family circle is wholesome and elevating, tending constantly to awaken in all the members, both old and young, an increased love for the contemplation of the wondrous skill and wisdom of the great Creator."—R. F. HAMILTON.

PREFACE.

THIS GUIDEBOOK contains the enumeration and description of nearly all the animals that have been or are on exhibition in the New York Aquarium. We have omitted only the mammals and birds that have lately been added to the collections, because it is intended to change them frequently, a few species of Parrotfishes (*Pseudoscarus*), Angelfishes (*Holacanthus*), and some Serranidæ that have been kept since last summer without identifying them. The technical names of the animals are made synonymous with those given by Gill and Verrill in their Washingtonian Reports. As a system of classification we have adopted that of Gunther in his Catalogue of the fishes in the British Museum. Much information has also been derived from the well-known works of DeKay and Jordan.

Our thanks are due to Mr. R. J. Edgar, Secretary of the Aquarium, who kindly gave us the benefit of his thorough knowledge of the English language, and to Mr. A. W. Roberts, Collector for the Aquarium, for many notes referring to the habits of the animals and for a list of those living in the tanks last summer.   H. DORNER.

NUMBERS CORRESPOND WITH THE NUMBERS
THE LABELS ON THE TANKS.

POPULAR DESCRIPTION

OF THE

INHABITANTS OF THE TANKS.

CLASS—MAMMALIA.

ORDER—*Artiodactyla.*   FAM.—*Pachydermata.*

1. THE HIPPOPOTAMUS OR RIVER HORSE
(*Hippopotamus amphibius*). This animal was captured on April 14th, 1875, by the collectors of Chas. Reiche & Bro., on an expedition to the White Nile. It was taken from its mother fifteen minutes after birth, the parent being killed. Three weeks prior to this time the natives had observed and pointed out to the hunting party a pregnant female, and it was at once decided to follow and watch her. When the animal had separated from the herd and selected a quiet, solitary place, the hunters, aided by spy-glasses, kept a careful and constant watch on her from a long distance, and so perfect were their arrangements, that only a quarter of an hour after the birth they were in possession of the young one. The reward of the natives consisted of the carcass of the mother, a prize they were highly satisfied with, as not only the flesh is well flavored and tender, resembling that of the hog, but the skin, the hoofs, and many other parts of the body are useful to them, in many ways. The hunters only claimed the skull, which was brought with the young animal to New York, on October 27th, 1875.

To feed and transport the baby hippopotamus through the deserts of Africa, twenty-five goats and four strong camels were employed, the former to provide it with their milk, the latter to carry it in a suitable tank between them. Its weight was about ninety pounds when captured, it being a female and not as heavy as a male, which latter, as has been seen in the London Zoological Gardens, weighs nearly a hundred pounds when born. After its arrival it was put under the care of Dr. Kohn, who succeeded in keeping the animal during these two years in perfect health and to whom it is attached to such a degree that it follows him like a dog wherever he goes. Its food consisted entirely of milk during the first three months of its stay in America, and was then changed to bread, cornmeal and vegetables. Hay it does not like much, refusing even common grass in summer; but it is very fond of a peculiar kind of short grass growing in the Western States, which it occasionally eats in considerable quantities

The Hippopotamus is a lazy, indolent animal ; sleeps many hours in the day and rests without interruption at night. It takes to the water naturally, when moderately warm, and it will enter reluctantly cold water when ordered. Last winter it occasionally bathed in water of $35°$ Fahr., its health being uninjured apparently. The thick skin and the layer of fat beneath is a sufficient protection against cold. Yet it must be stated that in cold weather its skin bursts into folds at the neck and sides, sufficiently deep to place one's finger.

When left alone, or when it perceives its keeper, it utters short, rough sounds. Even when it is not able to see him, and when separated from him by an opaque wall, it will smell his presence from a distance and act accordingly. All its senses are well developed.

It generally is obedient and can be guided by commands, but when frightened, or when its eyes are not sufficiently clear—an occurrence happening once in about a month —it is wild, treacherous, and not to be trusted. At such times it is useless to attempt to drive it or use a whip or to use force in any way; the big, unwieldy mass, now weighing about six hundred pounds, will easily overcome any temporary obstacle. When it expects food or when its keeper orders it, it will open its immense mouth and permit an inspection of its teeth, but generally it does not care much for strangers, snaps at them, and sometimes will tear the coat or pants of some careless visitor. At one time it even succeeded in pulling a watch and chain from the pocket of a person. It dislikes children, who should not be allowed to go too near the animal.

In October, 1876, it cast its front teeth, in the same manner as children do, the new ones absorbing the roots of the primary teeth, which, when fallen out, measure but a quarter of an inch in height. Since that time, the new teeth have grown considerably, particularly the two middle incisors of the lower jaw; the molar teeth appear to be very small, because the thick, fleshy gum covers the greater part of them. Its skin is almost naked, covered only by a few short, black hairs, but beset with numerous red spots, probably the dried secretion of the dermal glands. When it sweats the skin is covered with a kind of blood-red slime, the exact nature or purpose of which is unknown.

The Hippopotamus is considered the most valuable of all exhibited animals, and this is the first time that a specimen has been seen as tame and obedient to its keeper.

ORDER—*Pinnipedia.*   FAM.—*Phocidae.*

2. THE COMMON SEAL. (*Phoca vitulina.*) A lengthy description of these pets of the Aquarium is unnecessary. Everyone who has seen their fat supple bodies, their intelligent countenances, their curious flippers, and has observed their great ability in swimming and diving, has been pleased and amused with their antics both in and out of the water. They have learned to climb, to ring a bell, to answer questions by barking, to make their bows to the audience, etc.

3. THE BLADDERNOSE SEAL. (*Cystophora cristata.*) A young specimen of this interesting seal was kept alive in the spring of 1877 for eight weeks. Its peculiarity consist in a hood, or hollow bag, right over the nose, which can be blown up at will and made to resemble a cap or hat. Ours was a young male, with a small protuberance which was raised only under excitement. It was very ferocious, tried to bite whoever approached it, and died at last from refusal of food.

4. THE **NORTHERN SEA LION.** (*Eumetopias Stelleri.*) This large and powerful animal was brought from the western coast of North America, where it is found in herds. The extreme length of a male is said to be sixteen feet, but animals measuring twelve feet are seldom captured. Females generally are not half as large as males. Many thousands of them are slain annually; their skin is used for glue-stock, their blubber, consisting of a double coating separated by a thin layer of muscular tissue, yields oil, in average ten gallons from each animal; the long spires of their whiskers, sometimes eighteen inches in length, are exported to China, where they are manufactured into personal ornaments.

This Sea Lion has an elongated head and neck, the latter without the mane which is characteristic of the southern Sea Lion; its upper lip is projecting and bears strong flexible whiskers; its eyes are full of expression; its ears small, cylindrical at the root, tapering to a point, and covered with short, fine hair. The teeth are strong, glistening and white. As in other Seals, the body resembles more a flexible bag filled with fat and meat than the body of an animal with a bony skeleton. Its flippers are encased with a sort of thick shagreen, and are extremely long, the fingers project far over the horny claws so that the flippers appear in a very peculiar way when the animal uses them to clean its skin. Besides, they act in a threefold manner, as legs, feet, and fins. The color of the body is varying; dark brown, reddish brown, dull or light yellowish gray.

The Sea Lions are found from the Galopagos Islands to the extreme north, and extend westward to the eastern coast of Siberia. They congregate in large herds on the islands and along the coast during the pupping season, which lasts three or four months in summer. During this time they feed very little; the males are most lively, bark and roar terribly so as to drown the noise of the heaviest surf, and fight desperately with each other, mutilating their bodies and not unfrequently disabling some of them from further association with their companions. In such strifes the ultimate victor has the supreme control over the whole herd or company. Both sexes unite in caring for the young, which at first have great aversion to the water; teach them their various movements and habits, and to capture their prey. At the close of the season, in September or October, they return to the sea, where they roam in all directions in quest of food, consisting of fish, mollusks, crustaceans, and seafowl, particularly gulls.

The whalers kill them with rifles, aiming at the ear—on other parts of the body the ball has but little effect—sometimes they succeed in cutting off their retreat to the sea and then dispatch them with clubs and spears.

ORDER—*Cetacea.*

5. THE BOTTLENOSE DOLPHIN (*Delphinus tursio*). A specimen measuring eight feet in length was captured in the neighborhood of New York and kept alive for nearly two months.

6. THE WHITE WHALE (*Delphinapterus leucas*). The effort made in the early history of the Aquarium to place one or more white whales on exhibition, was met by many serious obstacles, and only by the utmost pluck and perseverance was the enterprise successful. In the first place, it involved the outlay of considerable capital with the utmost uncertainty of any favorable results; while secondly, there were innumerable difficulties and dangers to be met and overcome.

Early in the spring of 1876, Captain Zack Coup, started on the perilous journey. His route was via Quebec and down the north shore of the St. Lawrence. The mode of travel was by sleighs as far as they were available. Afterwards it was by sleds drawn by a hardy breed of dogs, and on snow-shoes. These appliances being all arranged at Quebec, Captain Coup and his fellow-travelers were soon on the confines of an uninhabited region of snow, the only sign of life being an occasional wolf, or fox. Nothing beyond the usual incidents of travel, which consist of numerous upsets in the snow, and interviews with hunting parties of peaceable Indians, occurred on the way. The fishing coast was finally reached and an island in the lower St. Lawrence was selected as the headquarters of this perilous adventure. It being in advance of the season when the whales descend to the coast of Labrador, Captain Coup availed himself of the time to make his excavations and enclosures. These are the means of capture and safe keeping, and they are built between high and low tide,

so that the huge animal is in bondage before he knows it, and entirely free from injury. Two being secured, early in May, the work of preparation for their removal to New

York began. Huge and strongly-built boats were made and thickly padded with sea-weed; the Whales transferred thereto, were shipped on board of a schooner and brought to Quebec. Thence they were removed to an Express car and brought by the Grand Trunk Railway to Portland, Maine; one more transfer to a steamer, and the living and curious burden was on its way to New York.

Thus was settled the practicability of handling Whales for aquarial purposes, and subsequent expeditions so far succeeded as to bring as many as fourteen in all. It is however a too costly enterprise to continue, and the proprietors feel that even more than a reasonable expectation on the part of the public has been gratified, and that in discontinuing for a time the exhibition of Whales they will be free from the imputation of indifference either as to their own duty, or to the gratification of public curiosity and scientific examination.

The first two Whales arrived in New York, in May of last year, and were the occasion of great excitement and curiosity. But a greater ovation was given when two others were brought to the Sea Side Aquarium at Coney Island last summer. The Aquarium there was not yet formally opened to the public, but the number of employees and laborers called together to receive and escort these huge animals, was large enough to crowd the place. Two big boxes, each containing one whale, were carefully carried inside by twenty-four men, one of the sides of each box was knocked out, and the animals were rolled in over thick layers of sea-weed. Before they were placed in the water, they behaved as quietly as a turtle nailed to the deck of a ship. They breathed regularly through the big spout-hole on the upper end of the head, but neither opened their mouth nor moved their tail or fin, and the big, unwieldy body looked almost like a corpse. The grayish-white skin was scratched and torn in many places, and a look both at the big animal in its narrow box and at the gang of rough, weather-beaten men that formed its escort plainly told of the hardships and fatigues which they must have undergone.

Both whales and men were happy and contented indeed, when the transfer to the tank was over. The whales showed plainly they were satisfied and at ease, and though they could not give vent to their joy by jolly cheers, as the men did, they made noise enough by a lively splashing of the water with their powerful tails and loudly throwing out the air through their spout-holes. Soon the surface of the water was covered with numerous fragments of the skin, and a few days later the whales appeared in an entirely new covering, of a lighter color than before. As long as they lived in the big tank of the Aquarium, they kept together, always swimming alongside of each other. They never changed their position. One of them was at the outside of the circle all the time, the other at the inside of it. They never turned around so as to swim their way backwards; regularly, as the hands of a watch, and in the same direction as this, they moved around their tank. Even at night it never could be observed that they rested or swam slowlier than usual, but, on the contrary, as soon as it was dark, they were more lively than before. It does not seem that they ever sleep.

The only change in their habits is seen when a fresh supply of eels, their regular food, is thrown in. Then they begin to dive after them and chase them; keep longer under water, and spout more vigorously than before.

Another change was observed in one of the Whales on a Sunday morning. The animal was moving slowlier than usual, and when it came to the surface to spout, the accompanying sound was loud, harsh and disagreeable. It resembled the breathing sound of a man who has an obstacle in his throat and endeavors to throw it out. The Whale is hoarse, he has got a cold, was the general impression. This continued about two hours, when the sound grew less noisy and slowly changed to its normal condition. Exactly three weeks later, on another fine Sunday morning, the same animal seemed to be extremely weak. For the first time it really ceased to move or moved very slowly, at the same time being unable to keep its balance, and turning a little on its side, just as seen in fish when they are weak and dying. The other Whale soon began to perceive that something unusual and alarming was going on. At first he swam a little slowlier, so as to be always near his companion, but when even then he found himself alone, as the other one did not move at all, he made a small circle through a quarter of the tank so as to come up with him again. Sometimes he dived right under the sick companion—a behavior never seen before by any one present—so that his back coming up really touched the belly of this one to raise and support it.

The spectacle of the dying Whale and the touching assistance of his companion attracted a great many visitors, and every change in the behavior of the two was watched with anxiety. Two hours passed, when a change to the worse was observed. The sick Whale turned completely over and swam on his back. Endeavoring to gain the old position, he used up all the strength which was left to him, and the visitors were right in saying that this was his death struggle. After repeating this three times, and every time trying harder, but with less success, to regain his lost balance, he ceased to move and spout. The Whale died exactly at noon, July 15.

At a post-mortem examination it was found that the cold which the Whale had three weeks before, was the cause of his death. The big lungs were congested and unable to contain the quantity of air necessary for the sustenance of life.

It may be interesting to mention that the Whale was found to possess two large stomachs, the first one lined on the inside with a great number of compound warts, the second one smooth. Both are connected three inches below the end of the gullet, so that the first stomach may be regarded as a kind of *cæcum* or blind-gut. There were found some fragments of sea-lettuce and buccinum-snails in this stomach, and it is very likely that it serves as a receptacle for vegetable food, which is changed here in about the same way as in the first stomach of ruminant animals.

The remaining whale did not show any signs of weakness. It was lively and hungry as ever, and soon was the only captured living white whale in America. All the others, that had been shipped from Labrador to Cincinnati, Chicago, Rockaway and New York were dead.

When the season at Coney Island closed, the proprietors of the Aquaria, Chas. Reiche and Bro., decided to ship this animal, that had lived longer and was more vigorous than any of the rest, to the other side of the Atlantic. On Sept. 15th, it was brought on board the Bremen Steamer, carefully packed in the same manner as on its first shipment and under care of Capt. Zack. Coup, who had directed all whaling expeditions of the Aquarium; and a fortnight afterwards all prominent papers in Europe brought the astonishing news of the arrival of a living white whale in England. It was transported to the Royal Aquarium in London, where it expired four days after its arrival.

REPTILES.

TURTLES.

Reptiles with the body enclosed between two large shields, one on the back, the dorsal shield; the other opposite, the ventral shield. Both shields are composed of many small plates, which either overlap each other, like the scales of fishes, or meet in a seam or suture. Every plate consists of an outer layer of horn and an inner layer of bone, the latter of which is firmly connected with the spinal column and the ribs. Turtles have no teeth, but their jaws are encased in horny sheaths, usually with sharp cutting edges.

7. THE LEOPARD TORTOISE. (*Testudo pardalis.*) Several large and heavy specimens of these were brought by the collectors of Chas. Reiche and Bro. from South Africa, and deposited in the Aquarium. They are objects of curiosity and interest, as they gently and harmlessly move around among visitors. They feed on cabbage and other vegetables.

8. THE COUI. (*Testudo radiata.*) Smaller than the preceding species of the tortoise, in company with which it was imported from Africa. It walks about the floor of the Aquarium, and is admired for the beauty of its shell, which is hemispherical, with flat, grooved, yellow-rayed shields. Length six to twelve inches. Madagascar.

9. THE SPOTTED TORTOISE. (*Geoclemys guttata.*) Shield black brown, with round yellow spots. This is a small turtle, not exceeding in length five inches, and found abundantly in adjacent streams and ponds. On warm days it is seen on rocks and logs, basking in the sun, suddenly slipping into the water on the approach of real, or supposed danger. It feeds on small animals, and buries itself on the approach of winter in the mud at the bottom of ponds.

10. **THE PAINTED TORTOISE.** (*Chrysemis picta.*) This is the handsomest of the fresh-water tortoises in North America. Its shell is smooth, with yellow lines along the sutures; its head has yellow lines along the sides. It is a timid, inoffensive animal that feeds on insects and small amphibians. Length five to nine inches. Canada to Verginia; in ponds, never in running water.

11. **THE SALT-WATER TERRAPIN.** (*Malaclemis concentrica.*) Upper shell oval, the plates with numerous deeply impressed concentric lines, lower shell reddish or orange, with irregular hoops or rings; head, neck and legs dull bluish ash, with numerous black spots. This terrapin is well known and esteemed for its savory flesh. Length five to seven inches. New York to Florida.

12. **THE SNAPPING TURTLE.** (*Chelydra serpentina.*) As the name indicates, this turtle is not so sluggish and patient as its relatives, but on the contrary, it is ferocious and will snap at almost everything within its reach. Its neck is long and very flexile; its beak has a hooked upper jaw and sharp, cutting edges, and the animal is enabled to move its head around and reach almost to the middle of its back. It feeds on frogs, fishes and waterfowl. Its upper shell has three strong keels; its tail a central series of compressed tubercles. Length two to four feet. United States.

13. **THE MUSK TORTOISE, or STINK-POT.** (*Aroma chelys odoratum.*) A very small turtle with a brown shell and low stripes along the sides of the head. It lives in the mud of ponds and ditches, is usually coated with mud and aquatic plants, and emits a disagreeable odor. Length two to four inches. United States.

14. **THE MUD TORTOISE.** (*Kinosternum pennsylvanicum.*) Upper shell olive brown and vaulted; lower shell yellow or orange; jaws hooked; tail with a horny point. It inhabits ditches and muddy ponds, preys on fish, and has a strong, musky smell. Length four inches. Canada to Florida.

15. THE SOFT-SHELLED TURTLE. (*Platypeltis ferox.*) Shell cartilaginous on its margin, dark slate colored and spotted. It feeds on fish and small amphibians, and is said to be more inclined to bite than other species of turtles. Length eight to ten inches. United States.

16. THE GREEN TURTLE. (*Chelonia viridis.*) Everybody is familiar with the grotesque form of the turtles, and whoever watches a land-tortoise slowly crawling on its elephantine feet, may well be inclined to take these animals for neglected step-children of nature. But now look at the turtle in its fluid element! How easily does the water carry its ponderous mass, how quickly does the animal divide the dense element, and how suitably does the form of its body seem to be adapted to the movement of swimming! The tortoise of the land and the turtle of the sea are very dissimilar brothers indeed; unlike in faculties and habits, in mode of living, and in mastering or utilizing the surrounding circumstances. It is easy to comprehend that the slowly-moving land tortoise can get its living only from vegetation, while its roving relative feeds on animals. The former are scarce and of large size, while the latter abound in rivers and seas, and occur in all dimensions, from the size of a dollar up to the bulk of five hundred weight. The learned naturalist of the British Museum, John Edward Gray, knows only thirty different species of the land tortoise, against five hundred and twenty seven of those that are found in rivers and seas.

Nowhere is the perfect adaptation of the form of the turtle to the element in which it lives better understood than in an aquarium. The large, flat, oar-like forelegs, situated just at the heaviest part of the body are the chief motors, and the flat body, resembling in its form that of water beetles, rays, or flat fish, glides by their means easily and continuously through the water.

The Green Turtle is the largest and best known of all marine turtles. Its length is from two to five feet, and its weight from a hundred to a thousand pounds. The qualities of its meat are better understood and appreciated in a restaurant than in a guide-book.

CROCODILIA.

17. THE ALLIGATOR. (*Alligator mississippiensis.*) This species of Crocodile is found in great numbers in the Southern States. When full grown it is fifteen feet long, but it seldom reaches this length, because of the general hostility with which it is pursued and killed.

The Alligator, and other Crocodiles, constitute one of the most peculiar groups of animals living. They are one of those interesting intermediate links between the extinct giants of the primitive world and the present creation. They also approach the mammals in many parts of their organization. Their lungs are limited to the chest, which is separated from the abdomen by an imperfect diaphragm; the chambers of the heart are divided so as to prevent the mixture of the two kinds of blood; the vertebræ of the neck bear ribs making the lateral movement of this part of the body nearly impossible; and the development of their eighty conical teeth is unique. Each opens on its interior end and closely fits into an elongation of the jaw. From time to time a new tooth grows from below gradually lifting the old one, which is partly absorbed, the remainder being thrown off. Pieces of the old teeth are often seen in connection with the new ones. As this change of teeth continues throughout life, the opinion of the ancients, that the Crocodile had as many teeth as there are days in the year, is still short of the truth.

LIZARDS.

18. THE HORNED FROG. (*Phrynosoma orbiculare.*) This animal is called a frog, sometimes a toad, and, if a learned friend is near by, he will tell us that even their scientific name, *phrynosoma*, means "body of a toad." Yet even this designation is a misnomer, since the frog, or toad, never has scales and plates like this animal. It is only the *shape* of its body, which is flat and broad like a toad, that gave origin to its name. In fact it is a lizard.

Its flat body is covered with spines, which are especially prominent at the neck, resembling the collar worn by hounds in Germany when hunting wild boars and wolves. Probably nature had, in furnishing to the frog these spines, the same design as man has in giving them to the hounds, namely, protection from the teeth of their enemies. As to its habits it is inactive, lying all day long without any attempt to move, and but seldom taking food.

19. THE GLASS SNAKE, STUMPFOOT or SHELTOPUSIK. (*Pseudopus Pallasii.*) A native of Dalmatia, Austria. A very general popular fallacy prevails as to the true nature of these animals. Their snake-like appearance and locomotion favor this, and yet they present several essential differences from the snake. They have eyelids like the lizard, the snake has none; their teeth are not hooked like those of the snake, and on close inspection two small feet are discernible near the root of the tail. These structural peculiarities place them more among lizards; and that assumption is greatly strengthened by the manner in which these animals feed. They eat as a lizard does, and after the following fashion : a live mouse being placed in the box, it is caught by the head, and its body is pressed against the box ; its tormentor and destroyer meanwhile revolves with such rapidity as to benumb or stupefy it, and twists its body like a piece of string. The prey is then dropped, but still kept in view, that the tormenting and destructive process may be repeated until the last sign of life has disappeared. The mouse, now dead, is eaten as it would be by any other lizard large and strong enough for this purpose.

SALAMANDERS.

20. THE BLACK SALAMANDER. (*Desmognathus nigra.*) Uniformly black, sometimes with small white spots on the sides. Tail compressed and finned. Length four to six inches. Shallow waters in Pennsylvania and New York.

21. THE RED SALAMANDER. (*Spelerpes ruber.*) Vermilion red, with numerous dark dots. Usually found under stones in shallow streams. Length four to six inches. Eastern States.

22. THE TIGER SALAMANDER. (*Amblystoma tigrinum.*) Brown, with many yellow spots; body thick and strong, head long and narrow, occasionally it is found in hollow decayed trees. Length six to eight inches. United States, east of the Rocky Mountains.

23. THE AXOLOTL. (*Siredon pisciformis.*) A most interesting salamander, a native of Mexico, about nine inches long, with a broad head and a crested tail. It has three external gills on each side of the neck which separate into many branches and periodically flap backwards and forwards. Its color is dark brown. The specimens on view in the Aquarium were received from Europe.

The Axolotls were introduced into Europe in 1864 by the *Jardin d' Acclimation*. Five males and one female were placed on exhibition, and from them about 600 young were raised. After seven months, when nearly full grown, some remarkable changes took place in one of them. The large external gills disappeared almost entirely, the crest on the back and tail passed away, the head became narrower and more pointed, and light spots appeared on the dark body and limbs. Thus nearly the same changes took place in this animal which had been seen a number of times in the common Tritons, or Salamanders of Europe and America. Some weeks later a few more underwent the same transformation, until nine of them had assumed the ultimate form. In the next year (1866) five specimens out of a thousand exhibited the same extraordinary development, and a few more were observed in the next year.

Thus the supposition of some naturalists, before the evidence given by Dumeril that the Axolotl was really the larval form of some unknown Salamander, was established. Cuvier, long before 1865, made the following remark: "I am obliged to place the Axolotl among the genera with permanent gills, because a great many persons testify that it does not lose the same;" and Baird, the well-known leading naturalist of this country, said that the appearance of the Axolotl was so very larval as to exclude any doubt of its real nature, it being no evidence against this assertion that the perfect animal had not yet been found.

The extraordinary facts in the natural history of this animal are not the changes already described, for a similar transformation is regularly observed in a great many other salamanders, frogs and toads, but its taking place in such a few instances, and, chiefly, its power of reproduction in the larval form, an attribute belonging with hardly an exception to the last and highest form of animal life.

24. THE HELLBENDER. (*Menopoma alleghaniensis.*) This is the largest of amphibious animals found in the United States. It is slate colored, has a broad head with very small eyes, a depressed body lined with a prominent fold at its side, and a long, broad,  and depressed tail. It seldom comes to the surface of the water, though it has no gills; it breathes through its skin and lungs. Length one to two feet. Eastern States.

PROTEANS.

25. THE EUROPEAN PROTEUS. (*Proteus anguineus.*)

This animal is only found in subterranean lakes in Krain, (Austria). When first received their eel-like bodies were of a yellowish-roseate color. They manifested an extreme sensitiveness to light and sought concealment from it behind the rocks as soon as they were placed in the tank. Their graceful form makes them especially interesting to visitors. Their head is long and flat; their legs short and slender, the fore-feet ending in three, and the hind-feet in two toes, without nails or claws. Like the Axolotls, they have external gills of a bright red color. Their eyes are extremely small, and entirely concealed beneath the skin, so that it is impossible for them to get distinct impressions of form by sight. Yet they are affected by the light, and very probably their whole skin is sensitive to its delicate touch. This seems to follow, firstly, from their constant anxiety to get out of the light and remain in perfect darkness; and, secondly, from the fact of the light colored skin changing to black when exposed to daylight In about three months this change is accomplished. At first some dark spots make their appearance, and finally a bluish black color covers the entire body, except the belly and the under side of the compressed tail.

In some Aquaria animals of this species have been kept for more than two years without taking food. Dr. Mettenheimer killed two Proteus which he had kept entirely without food for two years and two months, and it surprised him to find in the stomach of one of them two living intestinal worms. The specimens in the Aquarium do not show any such abstemiousness. They devour earthworms and other food with avidity, displaying their greatest activity, however, when water insects and small crustacea, such as Gammarus and Daphnia, are placed in the tank. Then they cross the tank in every direction, snapping and catching the insects without once being impeded in their rapid progress. It appears that only when these insects are moving, the Proteus become sensible of their presence.

26. THE MUD PUPPY, or PROTEUS. (*Menobranchus lateralis.*) Like the Austrian Proteus, it has external gills which are persistent during life. It is brown, more or less spotted. Its head is broad and depressed, the tail high and compressed. It feeds on crustaceans, shells, and fishes. Length one to two feet. Eastern States.

FISHES.

SUB-CLASS—TELEOSTEI.

ORDER—*Acanthropterygii.* FAM.—*Gasterosteidæ.*

27. THE COMMON STICKLEBACK. (*Gasterosteus aculeatus.*) This little lively fish is very interesting in the care of its eggs and brood. The *male* fish builds a round nest with waterplants and, after the female has deposited the eggs, is constantly close by, moving the pectoral fins in such a way as to drive a current of water through the nest. Sometimes the female, or other Sticklebacks, try to interrupt him, to enter the nest, and to devour the eggs, but the watchful and courageous male maintains a successful fight and keeps them at a safe distance from his charge. During the time of incubation it feeds very little, and yet is more lively and more brightly colored than at any other time. If the young ones fall out of the nest, the male takes them into his mouth and returns them.

28. THE TWO-SPINED STICKLEBACK. (*Gasterosteus biaculeatus.*) Blackish, two large spines in front of the dorsal fin; the ventral spine with a spinous process at the base.

29. THE NEW YORK STICKLEBACK. (*Gasterosteus noveboracensis.*) The sides of the body and tail are entirely covered with a series of scaly plates. The ventral spine is very long.

FAM.—*Berycidæ.*

30. THE SQUIRREL. (*Holocentrum sogho.*) This is a very handsome fish with an elegant shape, and a reddish color that exceeds in brightness and splendor even that of the Goldfish. Its body is elongated and slightly compressed; its head is well proportioned, with prominent spines at the operculum; its fins are large and have beautiful outlines. It swims quickly and vivaciously. G. Brown Goode, the author of several works on Bermuda fishes, calls it one of the most conspicuous of the denizens of the rock pools in the Bermuda Islands. Their voracity, he says, is very great, and the tyro in angling usually finds his first prize to be a Squirrel. The local name refers to a grunting noise uttered by them, which resembles the bark of a squirrel.

FAM.—*Percidæ*.

31. THE YELLOW PERCH. (*Perca flavescens*.) Olive, sides yellowish with broad dark bars. This fish is the type or representative of the Percidæ or Perch family. It is very voracious, lively and strong, and will bite at almost any kind of bait. It differs very little from the European Perch, having a brighter hue and being a trifle less in height. Owners of Trout tanks are anxious to keep the Perch clear of them, as they destroy the Trout in great quantities. Fresh waters, United States, chiefly northward and eastward.

32. THE STRIPED BASS. (*Roccus lineatus.*, A fish of the Perch family, equally prominent for its beautiful shape and color, and its gamey character and savory meat. It is bluish black, silvery on its sides and beneath. Along each side are from seven to nine black parallel stripes. "This fish," says Genio C. Scott, "the fish of fishes, par excellence, affords good sport with light tackle when its weight is but half a pound; and it tries both the metal and skill of an angler after it rises to the ponderous importance of ten pounds, though it is said to attain to the weight of nearly a hundred. For muscular power the striped bass equals the salmon, but it lacks the caudal power for leaping, which is so palpable in the form of a salmon."

The striped bass is not given to wandering or vagrancy, but is always found near the tidal waters of the rivers between Portland and Norfolk. In November it shoals and congregates in brackish waters, where also its eggs are deposited. It has successfully been confined to fresh water, though deteriorated in form and lustre.

33. THE WALL-EYED PIKE, or YELLOW PIKE PERCH. (*Lucioperca americana.*) A large, handsome and savory fish, the form of which somewhat resembles that of

a pike though it is a true perch. It is yellowish grey with numerous dark spots; its eye is very large and prominent. Length twelve to eighteen inches; weight up to fifteen pounds and over. Great lakes and western rivers.

34. THE BLACK SEA BASS. (*Centropristis atrarius.*) This favorite fish is found along the Eastern coast of North America, from Cape Cod to Florida. It comes to us in the beginning of May, and remains through the summer. It is a strong, heavily built fish, of a blueish, sometimes a greenish, black color, with large scales, the deeper colored edges of which give a regularly reticulated appearance to the whole surface of the body, and a wide, leathery mouth, easily hooked and tenacious to hold.

It is regarded as one of the most savory and delicate fishes of the season, particularly excellent for chowder. Its meat laminates in compact flakes, and is more succulent and delicate in taste than that of the Cod. "The Sea Bass, Porgee, and Tautog banks, along the coast of New Jersey," says Genio C. Scott, "form one of the attractions of Long Branch, and they are a real blessing to the members of the hand-line committee, who realize in them a cheap relaxation from business and the lassitude caused by too constant work in a city during the heat of summer."

35. THE HAMLET OR GROUPER. (*Epinephelis striatus.*) A remarkable characteristic of this fish is its ability to suddenly change its colors. Generally it is light slate-colored, with many broad cross-bands and some black spots around the eye, but when touched or frightened, it quickly assumes a darker hue, from gray to dark chestnut. It is a very common fish in Bermuda; is caught there in great quantities, kept in artificial ponds along the shore, and fed on fish and lobsters.

"The Devil's Hole," says G. BROWN GOODE, "is a large natural pool near the centre of the main island. Here a large number of Groupers may usually be found confined, and the place is much visited by strangers. At feeding time, when one looks into the clear waters of the pool nothing can be seen but an array of open mouths. When the food is thrown in, a scene of indescribable commotion and splashing occurs. They are very fierce, and rush savagely at anything which looks eatable. I have seen two large ones, each four feet in length, seize the opposite ends of a cuttle-fish arm, tugging for several minutes at the tough morsel before the question of ownership could be decided."

The young fish are called Hamlets, but, after reaching a length of eighteen or twenty inches, are known as Groupers, which is a corruption of the Portugese *Garoupa*, the name of a similar fish found at Madeira.

36. THE HIND. (*Epinephelis guttatus*.) A very handsome fish, common in Bermuda, where specimens two feet in length are often met with in the markets. It is brownish or rosy-white, with numerous small circular spots of deep rose color, which are probably the origin of its popular name. When kept long in a tank with plenty of light, its color fades. It is also recorded that specimens from the "White Water," where there is a bottom of white sand, are nearly white, while others have a dusky reddish-brown color.

37. THE ROCK FISH. (*Trisotropis undulosis*.) A large fish, attaining a length of five feet, and known as one of the choicest table-fishes in Bermuda. Its color is brown, mottled with large irregular spots and lines of brownish-violet. The Hamlet, Hind and Rock Fish belong to a group of fishes which are normally hermaphrodite, each fish after maturity carrying milk and roe at the same time.

38. THE YELLOW-TAIL. (*Oxyurus chrysurus*.) A small fish with large fins. It is greenish olive, with oblique streaks above the lateral line and some shining golden bands along the sides. Bermuda Islands.

39. THE GRAY SNAPPER. (*Lutjanus caxis*.) This is a very common fish in Bermuda, with a low, elongated, dark grey body. It is cunning and dexterous, and has, from its ability to avoid all contrivances for catching it, gained the nick-name of "Sea Lawyer." It attains a length of four feet, and is said to be one of the most delicious of food-fishes.

40. THE FRESH WATER BASS. (*Centrarchus æneus*.) A handsome and savory fish found abundantly in the

great lakes and in the larger streams in the western counties of New York State. It is greyish brown, and each scale has a dark centre. The anal fin has five or six strong spines.

41. THE BLACK FRESH WATER BASS. (*Centrarchus fasciatus.*) A fish twelve to fifteen inches long and common in the great lakes. It is of a dusky blue or green color, often with transverse bands and conspicuous dark spots at the fins. The soft part of the dorsal fin is covered with scales at the base. The anal fin has but three spines.

42. THE SUNFISH. (*Pomotis auritus.*) A common but beautiful little fish that derives its proud name from its glittering colors. It is greenish olive with numerous red or orange spots; the operculum (gill cover) has a rounded, membranaceous, bright scarlet lobe above the angle. Great lakes and eastern rivers.

FAM.—*Pristipomatidæ.*

43. THE YELLOW GRUNT. (*Hæmulon xanthopterum.*) We have received a great number of different kinds of Grunts from the Bermuda Islands, where they are quite common and plentiful. They have an oblong, compressed body, a horizontal, wide mouth, blood-red inside, the usual number of fins, and a differently, but always handsomely colored body. The Yellow Grunt is easily recognized by its color. Its length is from six to twelve inches.

44. THE WHITE GRUNT. (*Hæmulon quadrilineatum.*) Light colored, with two brown and two broad golden bands along each side of the body. It is found in schools in the Bermuda Islands.

45. THE BLUE-STREAKED GRUNT. (*Hæmulon elegans.*) A beautiful fish, with many waving, light-blue, horizontal bands, edged brownish. Bermuda Islands.

46. THE MARGATE FISH. (*Hæmulon chrysopterum.*) This fish is nearly allied to the Grunts, but differs from

them by being larger in size and by its faculty to change color. Generally it is of a beautiful pearly-white, with two or three faint stripes along the body, but sometimes it suddenly assumes a darker hue, the stripes becoming almost black. Its length is from nine to eighteen inches. Bermuda Islands.

47. THE BLACK TRIPLE-TAIL or FLASHER. (*Lobotes surinamensis.*) A high bodied, strong fish. It is a foot or more in length, and is of a rusty blackish color. The anal fin and the soft part of the dorsal fin, are of equal development, both reaching to about the middle of the caudal and producing the appearance of a triple-tailed fish. It is rare on our coast, but is found in great numbers in the Carribean Sea, the Indian Ocean and the Chinese Seas.

FAM.—*Sparidæ.*

48. THE SILVER BREAM. (*Sargus argenteus.*) The color of this fish is a very brilliant silvery white, interrupted only by a black band across the back of the tail. Its body is high and compressed; the profile of its head is plain and oblique so as to form a pointed mouth. Its length is from six to twelve inches. It is common in Bermuda.

49. THE SHEEPSHEAD. (*Archosargus probatocephalus.*) A big, clumsy fish with about a dozen large, bare teeth, and five conspicuous blackish cross bands. The appearance of its mouth and teeth, the profile of its head, curved nose and forehead are sheep-like, whence the name. They are found in our waters during summer, when they are eagerly looked after as a delicacy. They return to the South in the fall. Length ten to twenty inches. Cape Cod to Florida.

50. THE RHOMBOIDAL PORGEE or SARGO. (*Lagodon rhomboides.*) Similar to the preceding, but smaller and more graceful. It has five dusky cross bars, like the Sheepshead, longitudinal stripes above the lateral line, and a black blotch at the origin of it. Length three to five inches. Cape Cod to Florida.

51. THE BIG PORGEE. (*Stenotomus argyrops.*) A brilliantly shining fish with a high compressed body, convex above. There are four to six strong conical canine-like teeth in the outer series of teeth of both jaws. This fish was formerly abundant in our waters during the summer season, and was brought in large quantities to the markets, where it commanded a high price. It has become scarce now. Length six to twelve inches. Cape Cod to Florida.

FAM.—*Squamipinnes.*

52. THE FOUR-EYED FISH. (*Sarothrodus bimaculatus.*) This is a very graceful and delicate fish, with a nearly circular outline, and a protruding and pointed snout. Its body is pearly-grey; the vertical fins are bright yellow; a black band runs across the eye. Its name has reference to a black eye-like spot on each side of the tail, which the fishermen believe to be a true eye. Brown Goode states that it is usually seen in sheltered coves, lazily swimming a few feet below the surface, under the shadow of some high rock. Its length seldom exceeds four inches. Bermuda Islands.

53. THE ANGEL FISH. (*Holacanthus ciliaris.*) This is a common fish in the West Indies and the Bermuda Islands, and is easily procured during summer; yet none more beautiful has ever been placed in our tanks and none that was regarded with as much pleasure and enthusiasm. It is one of those tropical creatures which nature seems to have endowed with a bountiful hand, and that awakens feelings of admiration.

No description can give an adequate idea of the grace and beauty of this fish. It must be seen to be appreciated. Its body is short and high; the dorsal and anal fins are very large, protruding at their anterior parts, thick at their base and covered with scales, so that they seem to be a continuation of the body. The scales are large, delicate brown with a shade of olive-green, and each of them is edged with a lighter tint. The chin, nape, upper eye-lid, base of the pectoral and ventral fins, and the margin of the dorsal and anal fins are bright cobalt-blue, with lines of the same color extending over the operculum. The caudal fin and the continuation or appendages of the longest spines of the dorsal and anal fins are bright yellow.

The motions of the Angel Fish are slow. It is seen in the sheltered parts of the coral reefs of the Bermuda Islands, lazily and gracefully swimming or floating a few feet below the surface. It feeds principally on coral-polyps. It attains a weight of four pounds, and is considered the best flavored fish in Bermuda.

54. THE BROWN ANGEL FISH. (*Holacanthus tricolor.*) We have received several specimens of this equally handsome and graceful fish from Florida. Its form and habits resemble those of the preceding species; its color is mainly dark brown, each scale being edged with a lighter color; the head and some markings are yellow. Its length is from six to fifteen inches.

55. THE BLUE-STRIPED ANGEL FISH. (*Holacanthus formosus.*) This is a small, dark-colored species, ornamented by four blue transverse bands over the body and a blackish ocular band, edged with blue. We had several specimens of this fish brought from Florida.

56. THE MOON FISH or THREE-TAILED PORGEE. (*Parephippus faber.*) The body of this fish is much compressed and elevated and has six dark vertical bands; the third dorsal spine is elongated, and the anterior portion of the dorsal and anal fins is protruding. It is a large and remarkable looking fish, of from five to eighteen inches. It is occasionally found in great numbers in our vicinity during the summer. Cape Cod to Florida.

FAM.—*Triglidæ.*

57. THE SEA-RAVEN or YELLOW SCULPIN. (*Hemitripterus acadianus.*) It is very difficult to give an exact idea of what a sea-raven is. If we say, it is the most ugly, fantastically comical, or funny-looking fish we ever saw, the description would not be understood, and if we would give the minutest details in an elaborate description, it would not be read. It must be seen alive in water to be appreciated.

Fishermen have a great aversion to it and regard its presence in their nets with a feeling little short of abhorrent disgust; some are even afraid to touch it, believing it to be poisonous, and yet it is an object of great curiosity to visitors.

The body of this remarkable fish is covered with appendages, the form of which is very variable. The color of some specimens is brown with darker spots, that of others, mottled like marble, or red, or bright lemon with white spots. There are no scales in its skin, so that when you touch or handle it, it feels like a soft, slippery, quivering mass of jelly-like substance. The sea-raven is often found in the vicinity of New York, but it is more abundant further north.

58. THE NORTHERN SCULPIN. (*Cottus grœnlandicus.*) A fish full of spines but without any scales. If attacked it spreads all the spines so that no animal can touch it without hurting itself. This species generally has circular white spots on the abdomen. Polar Regions to Cape Hatteras.

59. THE SLENDER SCULPIN. (*Cottus octodecim-spinosus.*) When taken from the water this fish spreads its head to twice its usual size by the distension of the branchial membrane, and presents rather a formidable appearance. The spine on the pre-opercle reaches the point of the opercle. Nova Scotia to Cape Hatteras.

60. THE SMOOTH-BROWED BULL-HEAD. (*Cottus mitchilli.*) The most common of this genus in the vicinity of New York. It is of a yellowish color, with confluent bars and blotches over the body; all the fins with interrupted black bars.

61. THE BANDED GURNARD OR SEA-ROBIN. (*Prionotus lineatus.*) A rather queer looking fish, with many spines and very large pectoral fins. In front of these fins there are three filaments or fingers, which can be moved separately and are used as feelers when it crawls over the bottom. It is a bottom-feeder, and not only devours various kinds of crustaceans but takes the bait off the hook of fishing lines, carefully avoiding the sharp steel points. Cape Hatteras to Florida.

62. THE WEB-FINGERED GURNARD. (*Prionotus carolinus.*) This is a larger and scarcer species than the preceding one. It is of a brown hue, clouded with a still darker color. The first dorsal fin has a black spot; the second is marked with oblique whitish streaks. Cape Cod to Florida.

63. THE FLYING ROBIN. (*Dactylopterus volitans.*) The pectoral fins of this queer looking fish are so largely developed that it is enabled to leap above water and soar after the manner of a bird, sometimes as far as two or three hundred feet. It is a handsome fish, but so curiously shaped as to make a description of it difficult of comprehension. Length about six inches. Newfoundland to Florida.

Fam.—*Sciænidæ*.

64. THE BIG DRUM. (*Pogonias chromis.*) A heavily built fish attaining to a large size and a weight up to eighty pounds. It is easily recognized by having about twenty cirri or beards beneath the lower jaw. It is found in our waters during summer, and feeds on mussels, clams and oysters, varying this food with crustaceans. In winter it is found in the South. The name is derived from a noise it produces resembling the distant sound of drums, probably caused by the strong compression of the expanded pharyngeal teeth upon each other, when they crush and grind the oystershells. The young of this fish are described as—

THE BANDED DRUM. (*Pogonias fasciatus.*) They resemble the old ones except in their color. Their surface shines silvery, and there are four to five blackish vertical bands extending down the sides.

65. THE KING FISH. (*Menticirrus nebulosis.*) A handsome fish, with seven oblique dusky bands descending from the back to below the lateral line, and a short barbel at the chin. It often lies on its side to rest, appearing to visitors as if sick or dead. It got its high-sounding name from the early English colonists, to designate the high esteem in which it was held as an article of food. Cape Hatteras to Florida.

66. THE LAFAYETTE FISH. (*Liostomus obliquus.*) A handsome fish, with fourteen to eighteen transverse, oblique bands over the back. Color whitish, shining purplish and silvery when the sun strikes it. The front of its head is nearly perpendicular. This fish happened to be in the vicinity of New York in almost incredible numbers in the summer of 1824, when "the great and good La Fayette" arrived in this city, and thus his name was unanimously given to the fish which was then considered entirely new. Since that time the Lafayette Fish is a permanent resident in our waters, but seldom in great numbers. Its length is from six to ten inches. Cape Cod to Florida.

67. THE RED or SPOTTED BASS. (*Sciænops ocellatus.*) A beautiful, well flavored fish with a low body. There are one or two conspicuous black spots at the root of the caudal fin. It is bluish above; the head, cheeks and shoulders are golden, with metallic reflections. Length one to three feet. Cape Cod to Florida.

68. THE WEAK FISH, or SQUETEAGUE. (*Cynoscion regalis.*) A fish with a long, slender body, bluish above, with darker oblique streaks, following the transverse series of scales. It visits our coast during the spawning season, which lasts from April to November. The best time to catch this fish is from June to October when the shad begin to disappear. The meat of small weak-fish is white and rather mealy; while of those weighing about ten pounds it is as flaky as that of a salmon.

Fam.—*Scombridæ.*

69. THE PILOT FISH. (*Naucrates ductor.*) This is a well known fish to mariners. It generally accompanies the shark, and receives its name from the supposition that it is their leader. Probably it feeds on the matter execreted and rejected by the shark. Its body is oblong and bluish

with five to seven dark vertical bands, and a keel on each side of the tail. Its length is from six to eighteen inches. It is found in all the seas of the temperate and tropical regions.

70. THE SUCKER FISH or WHITE - TAILED-REMORA. (*Leptecheneis naucrates.*) The most remarkable peculiarity of this fish is the flattened disk on the upper part of the head, into which the first dorsal fin is transformed. By means of this disk, which is composed of numerous transverse, cartilaginous, movable plates, the Sucker fastens itself to the bottom of ships or to the belly of fishes, such as large sharks. This serves the double purpose of enabling it to travel to great distances, and to get its nourishment from larger and stronger animals than itself. This will account for its location at points so remote from each other as China, Australia, and our own coast, which it could not reach except by adhering to ships. The ancient Romans, to whom this fish was well known, believed that a ship, to which a Sucker fastened itself, was unable to be moved. Its length is from twelve to eighteen inches.

71. THE HARVEST or DOLLAR FISH. (*Poronotus triacanthus.*) A gorgeously colored fish. Its sides are resplendent with brilliant metallic green, blue and golden hues. The body is much compressed and elevated; the dorsal and anal fins are low and long, and of equal development. It is similar in size and form to the horse-fish (No. 75), which it resembles in its dancing motion; the dorsal outline is equally rounded in its entire length, but it has no ventral fins like the horse-fish. Maine to Hatteras.

FAM.—*Carangidæ*.

72. THE HORSE CREVALLE. (*Carangus hippos.*) A beautiful and gorgeously colored fish with a much compressed and nearly elliptical body. The lateral line is armed on its posterior part with bony plates. Length six to nine inches. Cape Cod to Florida.

73. THE YELLOW MACKEREL. (*Carangus chrysos.* Similar to the former, but the body is lower, more elon-

gated, and the yellow color extends farther. Both fishes appear in our waters in August, and leave about the beginning of October. In confinement they are very delicate, and die when frightened. Length six to nine inches Cape Cod to Florida.

74. THE THREAD FISH or LONG ISLAND ANGEL FISH. (*Blepharichthys crinitus*.) The beauty of this little fish exceeds even that of the tropical fishes. Its body, which is not over six inches in length, has an almost circular outline, and is covered with a delicate skin, shining with the colors of mother-of-pearl The pectorals and the anal fin are elegantly shaped and of a silk-like appearance. But the most remarkable feature of this fish is the long, silk-like threads, the continuation of the spines of the dorsal and anal fins. These surpass the length of the body three to four times. The movements of this tender fish are very interesting. It keeps afloat near the centre of its tank, and moves carefully around so as not to hurt its long, floating threads. It is scarce in our waters, but is found during August and September on the Long Island coast. Later in the season it returns to the Caribbean Sea. The French colonists in the Antilles call it the "Shoemaker" (*Cordonnier*), probably because of the long threads which, at their ends, resemble pieces of white wax.

75. THE HORSE or MONKEY FISH. (*Vomer setipinnis*.) The body of this fish is much compressed and elevated; the back is nearly straight, abruptly descending above the eye and forming a concave profile. It is a beautiful, uniform silvery fish, swimming in a peculiar way. Each stroke of the long pectorals brings it suddenly upwards, but only to sink again the next interval, so that it seems to be in a kind of dancing motion. Length six to ten inches. Maine to Florida.

76. THE BLUE FISH. (*Pomatomus saltatrix*.) A well known and valued table-fish, bluish above, lighter beneath and on the sides. Its body is oblong and compressed. The cleft of the mouth is rather wide and the jaws contain a series of very strong teeth. Those caught in September and October are the most prized. They have a wide range in nearly all the seas of the tropical and temperate regions.

77. THE BLACK RUDDERFISH. (*Palinurichthys perciformis.*) An occasional visitor to our shores. Its body is oblong, elliptical and compressed; length nine inches. Color bronze black; eyes orange yellow. Maine to Cape Hatteras.

FAM.—*Batrachidæ.*

78. THE TOAD-FISH. (*Batrachus tau.*) An ugly fish without any scales, and covered with a thick coating of slime, so that the color does not appear with distinctness. Sometimes it is olive-green, mottled with brown; at other times it is brown, marbled with darker colors. The head is wider than the body. Generally this fish lies motionless at the bottom, half buried in the sand or in seaweed. It gets its food either by sucking in small marine animals, or by suddenly seizing smaller fishes within its reach. Its flesh is said to be well flavored when properly cooked. Length six to twelve inches. Nova Scotia to Florida.

FAM.—*Pediculati.*

79. THE ANGLER, SEA-DEVIL, FISHING-FROG, BELLOWS-FISH, GOOSE-FISH or MONK-FISH. (*Lophius piscatorius.*) This is a very ugly and repulsive looking fish. It seems to be nothing but head or rather mouth, with a small body attached thereto. The head is nearly circular in its outline, the cleft of the mouth occupying half of it. The teeth are large and numerous, and there are many small

barbels around the mouth. Its first dorsal fin consists of a few, separate, very long and flexible spines, which are in perpetual motion, and thus serve to attract its prey, while the fish is otherwise at rest on the bottom, half covered by sand and mud. Another peculiarity of its body are the stalked or pedunculated pectorals which clearly indicate their homology with the arms or forelegs of higher animals.

The Angler is not uncommon on our coasts. It has been caught off the battery in New York City, and is sometimes hauled up by the lines laid out for codfish, having swallowed one of the fish and being unable to get rid of hook and line. There have been exhibited in the Aquarium several specimens of this fish, and a large cast, made of one of them, shows all the remarkable features of their body; but unfortunately it seems to be almost impossible to keep them alive in the tanks for more than a couple of days.

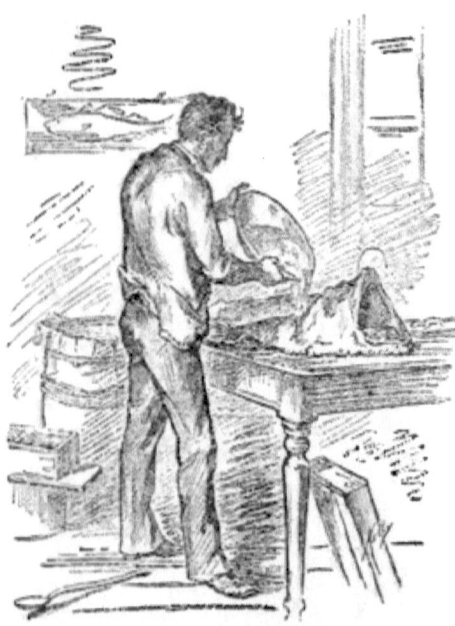

80. THE WALKING FISH. (*Pterophryne lævigata.*) This fish is a near relative of the Angler. Its pectoral fins are pedunculated so as to resemble the forefeet of a mammal, after the manner of which it uses them. It is a remarkable sight to see this curiously shaped fish quietly and slowly crawl along the bottom of the tank, placing one foot after the other with apparent cautious discernment. But for this peculiarity one might be inclined to

take the Walking Fish for a Sea-raven, the odd fringes and tossels of which are even more plainly conspicuous and numerous than in the raven. The whole body is covered with cutaneous tentacles; even parts of the fins are transformed into tufts branching off to the sides like fern leaves. The ground-color of the skin is yellowish, largely marbled with brown; round white spots are on the sides and belly. Specimens of this fish have been found in the Atlantic, the Indian and Chinese seas, north of Australia and in Polynesia. That exhibited in the Aquarium was caught near Newport, R. I., and presented by Mr. E. V. Lawter.

FAM.—*Blenniidæ*.

81. THE SEA WOLF. (*Anarrichas vomerinus*.) A fish three to five feet long, with an elongated body, long and narrow dorsal and anal fins, a high and compressed head, and large, ugly teeth in a wide mouth. It is said to be of a voracious and savage character, and marvellous tales are related by the fishermen of the strength and power of their jaws, exaggerations, probably, from its formidable appearance. Greenland to Cape Hatteras.

82. THE WRY-MOUTH, or GHOST-FISH. (*Cryptacanthodes maculatus*.) A rare and remarkably shaped fish, with an eel-like body and an oblong head, the lower jaw of which is directed upwards in a very conspicuous way. The name is derived from its sullen or wry-mouthed facial expression. It is of a reddish white color, with many irregular, bright, reddish brown blotches. Nothing is known about its habits. In confinement it tries to conceal itself, moves very little and probably feeds at night. Nova Scotia to New Jersey.

83. THE EEL-POUT, CONGER-EEL or LAMPEREEL. (*Zoarces anguillaris*.) A fish with a long and narrow body; the dorsal, caudal and anal fins connecting. The head is thicker and wider than the body; the mouth is situated at the lower side. Its color is dark olive, varied with dusky blotches. It is caught in company with the Cod. Length two to three feet. Newfoundland to Cape Hatteras.

Fam.—*Acronuridæ*.

84. THE DOCTOR-FISH. (*Acanthurus nigricans*) This fish derives its name from a movable, lancet-shaped spine, situated in a longitudinal groove on each side of the tail. It is dark-colored, with different, rather inconsistent markings of blue; its body is high and compressed. Its movements are quick and nervous, and when kept confined with other fish, they are subject to serious injury from its lancet. They are of such a chivalrous character that one Doctor-fish will even fight and kill another of the same kind Their length is from six to twelve inches. We had specimens of it brought from Bermuda.

Fam.—*Labyrinthici*.

85. THE GOURAMI. (*Trichogaster fasciatus*.) A small, but very handsome fresh-water fish from the East Indies, imported to this country by Messrs. Chas. Reiche & Bro. Their high and compressed body has many oblique, dark stripes. The abdominal fins resemble long bristles, and the anal fin is lined by vermilion dots.

Fam.—*Mugilidæ*.

86. THE STRIPED MULLET. (*Mugili lineatus*.) A slender fish with nearly a straight dorsal outline; head covered with large scales, shining with a greenish metallic reflection. Length six to eight inches. Cape Cod to Florida.

Fam.—*Pomacentridæ*.

87. THE COW-PILOT, or SERGEANT-MAJOR. (*Glyphidodon saxatilis*.) A short fish, not exceeding six inches in length, with an elevated body and five black cross bands in a golden-green skin. It very common throughout the West Indies, and frequents the sheltered waters in company with Parrot, Angel, and Four-eyed Fishes. It feeds on shellfish. Our specimens were brought from Bermuda, but did not long survive the change.

FAM.—*Labridæ*.

88. THE HOG-FISH. (*Lachnolæmus falcatus.*) This fish gets its name from its swine-like profile and dentition. Its body is compressed and elevated, its snout pointed, its dorsal spines protruding, and its skin resembles brown and red marble. When it swims, the dorsal spines and their long, streamer-like appendages or continuations give it a singularly graceful appearance.

It is very common in Bermuda and caught there in great numbers. It attains a length of thirty inches and a weight of twenty pounds; has a hard, white, exquisitely-flavored flesh, and ranges among the choicest of table-fish.

89. THE NEW YORK TAUTOG, or BLACKFISH. (*Tautoga onitis.*) Belongs to the family of *Labridæ* or Wrasses, so called from *labrum* or lip, which is protrusile in these fishes. These fishes live on rocky shores, and feed chiefly on mollusks. Their dentition is admirably adapted for crushing shells and crabs.

The Tautog has a compressed, oblong body, covered with small, adherent scales; its color is bluish black, with irregular darker blotches and bands. It is abundant on our coasts from April until late in the autumn, when it retires into deeper water. It weighs about two pounds, but is sometimes found weighing as much as ten pounds. It is a well-known, strong, savory fish, and is a great favorite with anglers, to one of whom (Isaac M'Lellan) we are indebted for the following accurately descriptive lines:—

> Wherever kelp and sea-weed cling
> To ramparts form'd of rugged rocks,
> The tautog finds a dwelling place,
> Deep down in waters at their base ;
> Or where a passing boat hath met
>   Its fate along the rocky shore,
> And, with its broken ribs and keel,
>   Lies rotting on the ocean floor—
> There, where the clinging shell and weed
>   Gather, and barnacles abound,
> The blackfish, seeking out their food,
> In numbers by the hook are found.

90. THE BERGALL or CUNNER. (*Tautogolabrus adspersus.*) A prettily shaped, lively and cunning fish, with

a row of sharp, cutting teeth in both jaws, covered by fleshy lips. Its colors are variable, more or less blue or brown, sometimes with dusky bars. The fishermen dislike this fish because it nibbles their bait. Length six to twelve inches. Newfoundland to Cape Hatteras.

THE SPOTTED BERGALL. (*Tautogolabrus uninotatus.*) This is apparently only a variety of the former. It has a black spot on the first two soft rays of the dorsal fin.

91. **THE SLIPPERY DICK.** (*Chærojulis bivittatus.*) This fish has its curious name from its ability to escape from the nets and pounds, or from the hand, by aid of its quickness in moving and its slippery surface. When caught and put into an open tank it tries to get out by jumping high above the surface. It is a small fish, about six inches long, with a straight upper and lower outline. Its surface is covered by brown, bluish and red spots and bands; the base of its dorsal fin is violet. It likes to hide itself, and at night to sleep among the pebbles or sand at the bottom of the tank, and so thoroughly does it conceal itself that hardly a spot of it is to be seen; but when disturbed it swims around lively and dexterously. The inhabitants of the Bermuda Islands do not eat this fish because they have a superstitious belief that they will lose all their hair after doing so

---

FAM.—*Gadidæ.*

92. **THE CODFISH.** (*Gadus morrhua.*) This is one of the most valuable of all fishes. It lives in deep water during the summer months, comes to the shores about the end of August, and remains in the vicinity of the land all winter. During this time many millions of them are caught. Their weight averages from five to fifteen pounds, but it is not uncommon to find specimens weighing forty or fifty pounds, and several trustworthy persons have reported the capture of cod of more than five feet in length and of a weight of over a hundred pounds. The number of eggs in one cod is simply enormous. In one instance the roe weighed seven and three-quarter pounds, and, on

a careful calculation, it was found to contain no fewer than 6,876,000 eggs. This explains how it is possible that the sea contains such a vast supply of this useful fish.

In 1865 it was discovered by Dr. George Ossian Sars, a famous naturalist of Norway, that the spawn of the cod and similar fishes floats on the surface of the sea during the whole period of its development, which is stated by him to occupy sixteen days. The eggs are almost transparent and resemble grains of boiled sago.

The Cod is found in countless schools in the northern parts of the Atlantic ocean, both on the American and European coasts, in greatest abundance, however, in the vicinity of New England and Newfoundland, as was known centuries ago. Those on the New England coast are said to be better than what are caught off Newfoundland. This was known as early as 1616. Capt. John Smith said in a report about them: "In the end of August, September, October and November, you have Cod againe to make Cor fish or Poore John : & each hundred is as good as two or three hundred in the New-found Land." Thomas Morton writes about the Cod at the coast of New English Canaan (New England), in 1636: "The coast aboundeth with such multitudes of Codd, that the inhabitants of New England doe dunge their grounds with Codd; & it is a commodity better than the golden mines of the Spanish Indies; for without dried Codd the Spaniard, Portugal & Italian would not be able to vittell of a shipp for the sea."

The food of the Cod is greatly varied and consists, according to the statement of Simeon F. Cheney, of crabs, scollops, and the jellies on the bottom. Larger Cod eat small flounders, small pollock and hake, small salmon, sea-perch, cunners, with other things found at the bottom of the water, but they always prefer the herring. Some come in schools and eat the herring spawn.

There are two varieties of the Cod, a smaller one, with a bright golden color, that lives mostly on the banks; and a larger one with a brownish color that is found on the shore. Some specimens of the former are almost as bright as goldfish. They are splendid to look at. "How unlike," says Frank Buckland, "how very unlike is a live cod to the flabby, big-headed creature one sees on the fishmonger's slab! The live Cod is an intelligent looking creature. True he has an immense mouth and great rolling eyes, but can't he swim! He goes as easily and as swiftly as an express train. A slight move of his tail and away he goes, darting like an arrow."

93. THE TOM-COD, or FROST-FISH. (*Microgadus tomcodus.*) A small and lively fish, found on our coasts at all times, but most abundantly after the first frost in the early part of winter. Its head is small and flattened above; its tail is long and slender. It is of dark olive green color, with irregular streaks and blotches. Length four to twelve inches. Newfoundland to Cape Hatteras.

94. THE HADDOCK. (*Melanogrammus æglefinus.*) Has, like the cod, a *barbel* at the chin, three dorsal and two anal fins. The abdominal fins are situated in front of the pectorals. It is distinguished from the cod by a lighter color, the jet black lateral line, and by the form of the first dorsal which is elevated and pointed.

The Haddock is not as common as the cod, though it comes to our markets by the hundred thousands, and is at times, particularly during summer, more easily obtained than the latter. It is inferior as an article of food, cannot be kept alive in the wells of the fishing smacks like the cod and is very difficult to keep alive in a tank.

95. THE POLLOCK, or COAL-FISH. (*Pollachius carbonarius.*) Similar to the cod and often taken in company with it. Its color is a dark blackish green; the fins are blackish brown. It has no barbel at the chin, or at most a very small one. Length one to three feet. Northern Atlantic, on the European and American coasts.

96. THE CODLING or SQUIRREL-HAKE. (*Phycis chuss.*) Reddish brown; the third ray of the first dorsal elongated; the filamentous ventrals almost half as long as the body. It is sometimes very abundant on our coasts. Length one to three feet. Newfoundland to Cape Hatteras.

97. THE SPOTTED CODLING. (*Urophycis regius.*) The color of this fish is pale brown, the lateral line very conspicuous, alternately black and white; the ventral fins

are reduced to a single long ray divided at its end. A singular habit of this fish is to lie for hours on its side, giving it the appearance of being sick. Length ten inches. Cape Cod to Cape Hatteras.

FAM.—*Pleuronectidæ*.

THE PLEURONECTIDÆ or FLATFISHES are common but very remarkable fishes, both in regard to their form and development. Most people would get the impression that Flatfishes lie on their belly, and that the darker colored back is directed upwards. This is a mistake, as a look at the fins and mouth will prove. The long dorsal and anal fins line the flat body, one each of the pectorals and abdominals is above, one below, and the jaws are placed as usual. Thus it is seen that Flatfishes lie on but one side. From this it follows that the sides are differently colored and, what is more remarkable, that both eyes are on one side of the head. These two anomalies do not exist in the young. Their form is symmetrical like that of other vertebrates : both sides are of the same light color, and one eye is on each side. But soon the eye on one side sinks into the head; a mark like a buttonhole appears at the opposite side, just above the other eye; the first one comes to sight again, and at the same time the change in the color of the sides is completed.

Flatfishes are found on a bottom of sand and gravel, their sides partly covered with it so that it is difficult to detect them. Only their large, protruding, opalescent eyes, which can be moved singly, are easily discovered. For moving through short distances they use parts of their dorsal and anal fins, leaning on them and thus slightly pushing their body. Their swimming consists of graceful, undulatory movements which are very interesting to see.

98. THE SPOTTED TURBOT. (*Lophopsetta maculata.*) Dark olive brown; body and fins with numerous black spots; the anterior rays of the first dorsal fin with membranous slips. This fish is considered a delicate article of food, but seldom found in our markets. Its length generally does not exceed fifteen inches, but sometimes specimens are caught that weigh twenty pounds. Cape Cod to Cape Hatteras.

99. THE COMMON FLOUNDER. (*Chænopsetta ocellaris.*) Olive brown; upper surface with spots, some of which are ocellated or encircled by a lighter ring. This savory fish is abundant on our coasts during summer. Its length is from twelve to eighteen inches.

100. THE RUSTY DAB. (*Chænopsetta oblonga.*) Nearly uniform brown; occasionally with spots; fins reddish brown; caudal fin angulated. Common along our sandy shores, being abundant in September and October. Length fifteen to twenty inches. Cape Cod to Cape Hatteras.

101. THE SPOTTED SOLE. (*Achirus lineatus.*) Color greenish brown, with numerous black lines and blotches. No pectoral fins. This species is very common, but too small to be of much value for the table. When kept in a tank with a sandy or muddy bottom, it buries itself out of sight. Length three to six inches. Cape Cod to Florida.

ORDER—*Physostomi*. FAM.—*Siluridæ*.

Numerous, mostly freshwater fishes, commonly called catfish, hornedpouts, and bullheads. They are easily known by their peculiar form: a broad head with thick lips and eight long, fleshy barbels, an unwieldy, thick and short body destitute of scales, and an adipose fin (a fin without rays or spines) situated between the dorsal and anal fins. They are sluggish in their movements, particularly when full grown, and secure their prey more by alluring it to their resting places at the muddy bottom than by swiftness. Some species do not grow over eight inches in length, others attain a very large size and a weight up to two hundred and fifty pounds. The Aquarium had one specimen weighing one hundred and sixty pounds.

102. THE COMMON CAT-FISH. (*Amiurus catus.*) Dusky, sides of the head greenish, those of the body cupreous. Caudal nearly even and rounded. Length six to twelve inches. Abundant in lakes and streams.

103. THE GREAT LAKE CAT-FISH. (*Amiurus nigricans.*) A large species from the great lakes; upper jaw longer than the lower; caudal fin deeply forked; color plumbaginous.

104. THE BROWN CAT-FISH. (*Amiurus pullis.*) Uniform dusky brown above, bluish white beneath. Abundant in the lakes of New York and eastward.

105. THE SEA-WATER CAT-FISH. (*Ailurichthys marinus.*) This is a handsome, swift and voracious fish, with two very long, fleshy barbels at the angle of the mouth, and two smaller ones at the chin. The dorsal fin is high and considerably curved ; the caudal is crescent shaped.

FAM.—*Salmonidæ*.

This family comprises more than one hundred and sixty species; most of them are very valuable fishes, and famous for both their game character and palatable flesh. They have an elongated, handsome body covered with a prettily colored, scaly skin, a naked head, and mouth with strong teeth, no barbels, and a small adipose fin behind the dorsal. In the spawning season they ascend the rivers, some of them as high as the region of permanent snow.

106. THE BROOK or SPECKLED-TROUT. (*Salmo fontinalis.*) Body olive, with blackish numerous red spots. It is an excellent and well known fish, affording high sport to the angler, and estimated in New York as the most relishable of all fishes. Their color varies nearly as much as their flavor ; those of clear mountain streams being considered the best. Length six to twenty-four inches. The rivers and lakes of British North America and the northern parts of the United States are abundantly stocked with them.

The Red-bellied Trout (*Salmo erythrogaster*) is a variety of the Brook Trout, with a reddish-orange abdomen.

107 THE LAKE-TROUT, SALMON-TROUT, or MACKINAW-TROUT. (*Salmo namaycush.*) Grayish in color and more or less spotted. Body stout and head very large. Length two to six feet. "His great size and immense strength alone" says Herbert, "give him value as a fish of game ; but when hooked, he pulls strongly and fights hard, though he is a boring, deep fighter, and, I think, never leaps out of the water like the true salmon or the brooktrout." Great lakes, north to the Arctic Seas.

108. THE CALIFORNIA SALMON. (*Salmo quinnat.*) Head pointed and large, dorsal line regularly arched; caudal deeply cut out. This is the most important salmon of the western waters, both in excellence and numbers. Many millions of its eggs have been transported during the last three years from California for distribution throughout the Eastern and Middle States. The Aquarium received in the

fall of 1876, 50,000 eggs from Spencer Baird, of the U. S. Fish Commission, which were successfully hatched and distributed in various adjacent waters. The same is done this season. The Pacific coast of North America, from San Francisco northward.

FAM.—*Esocidæ*.

109. THE GREAT LAKE-PIKE. (*Esox lucius var. estor.*) A beautiful fish, of an olive-green color, handsomely spotted with round yellowish spots as large as peas; each scale with a shining V-shaped mark opening sidewards. Length one to four feet. Great lakes and the headwaters of the Mississippi.

110. THE MUSKALLUNGE. (*Esox nobilior.*) Grayish with white spots; cheeks and opercles half bare. Length, one to six feet. Great lakes.

111. THE PICKEREL. (*Esox reticulatus.*) Green, with a network of brown streaks on the sides. Length, one to three feet. It is abundant in the streams of the Eastern and Middle States.

112. THE PIKE. (*Esox americanus.*) This fish is of a dark green color. Its sides are marked with about twenty distinct blackish bars. Its length is six to ten inches. It is found in the Atlantic streams of the Eastern and Middle States.

FAM.—*Cyprinodontidæ*.

113. THE SHEEPSHEAD LEBIAS. (*Cyprinodon variegatus.*) A small fish with large scales, one inch high and two inches long. The female has irregular and blackish vertical spots on the body. The male is without these spots. It lives in salt and brackish streams in the neighborhood of New York.

114. THE KILLIFISH. (*Fundulus diaphanus.*) This fish abounds in all our salt water creeks (which our Dutch an-

cestors called "kills") and bays. It is two to five inches long, has a small, rounded caudal fin, a short and high dorsal placed on the posterior part of the body, and is of a greenish color. The male has many broad cross bands; the female three more or less interrupted longitudinal bands.

FAM.—*Heteropygii.*

115. THE BLIND FISH. (*Typhlichthys subterraneus*). Several specimens of this interesting little fish were received from the famous Mammoth Cave in Kentucky. They are very small, not exceeding two inches in length, colorless, and without any ventral fins. Their eyes are rudimentary and of no use. On the head and sides of the body there are prominent ridges consisting of minute papillæ in which many nerves terminate. These papillæ are delicate organs of touch, enabling the fish to feel its way in the eternal darkness of its surroundings. They will live for several months in quiet, clear, and well aerated water.

FAM.—*Cyprinidæ.*

116. THE COMMON SUCKER. (*Catostomus teres*). A freshwater fish, having a long, rounded, tapering body, and thick, fleshy lips, of which the lower one is pendent. Length twelve to eighteen inches. It is abundant in our markets in autumn.

117. THE LONG-FINNED CHUBSUCKER. (*Carpiodes cyprinus*). This fish has a slight resemblance to the European Carp, and is often called by that name in this country. It has a whitish skin and large scales; the first rays of its dorsal fin are very much elevated and attenuated; the mouth is inferior. Length twelve to twenty inches. Eastern lakes and rivers.

118. THE GERMAN CARP. (*Cyprinus carpio*). A famous fish, from Germany, considered there as the most delicious and palatable of all fishes. Originally it was only found in some of the larger rivers, but many hundred years ago it was transported to artificial and natural ponds, and now it is spread over the larger part of Europe, some parts of Asia, and Australia. Those in our tanks were presented to the Aquarium by the well-known

fish culturist, Herr von Hessels, who imported several thousands of them, in the spring of this year, for the United States Fish Commission. Of the numerous varieties, found in Europe, he selected the so-called King Carp (*Cyprinus Rex Cyprinorum*), which is more highly prized than all others. It has but a few scales of enormous size, the larger part of its skin being naked. The Carps are very tenacious of life, easily endure changes of temperature, and will successfully feed on all kinds of vegetable refuse.

119. THE GOLD FISH. (*Carassius auratus*). No other fish is more widely distributed throughout the world than this. It was imported from China to England, by Philippe Worth, in the year 1728, was successfully bred and universally distributed. There are many varieties of this fish exhibited in the New York Aquarium, some with double anal or caudal fins, some black, red, silvery white, or spotted. The most renowned of all varieties is that described in the following section:

120. THE KINGIYO. This fish, together with seven others, was imported from Japan by Mr. Gill, of the firm of Martin, Gill & Co., large importers of tea from that country, and presented by him to the Aquarium. Too much cannot be said of the singular and unique beauty of this specimen. The sides of its thick and short body are resplendent with the most brilliant golden and pearly hues. The caudal and anal fins united are nearly the length of the entire body, resembling the most delicate silken tissue; affords a splendid view as it slowly and solemnly floats through the water. Many visitors have expressed the opinion that this is the most remarkable and beautiful fish they had ever seen.

121. THE LONG-TSING-YU, CHINESE QUADRUPLE TAIL, TELESCOPIC or DRAGON-EYED FISH. Four specimens of this valuable fish, which must be regarded as another variety of the Goldfish, were imported to this country by Messrs. Chas. Reiche & Bro. They have remarkably large, protruding eyes, which almost seem to be located outside of the head, and give to the small, lively, and gracefully-built fish a resemblance to the Hammerhead Shark. All our specimens came from China.

122. THE BLACK-NOSED DACE. (*Rhinichthys atronasus*). A small fish, found abundantly in the streams and rivulets of New York and adjoining States. It is from one to three

inches long, and is easily recognized by a black band that runs from the snout to the root of the caudal fin.

THE KINGIYO.

123. THE ENGLISH ROACH. (*Leuciscus rutilus*). Some specimens of this fish were brought to this country by Capt.

Mortimer, of the ship "Hamilton Fish," a gentleman of large experience and fine culture, and presented by him to the Aquarium. They belong to a genus that has representatives in Europe, Asia, and America. Our species has a silvery-white body, with red eyes and fins.

124. THE SHINING DACE. (*Leuciscus argenteus*). A handsome fish, with an elongated and silvery-white body. The scales are large, and have blackish membranes at their base. Length three to eighteen inches. New England and New York.

125. THE GERMAN TENCH or SCHLEIHE. (*Tinca vulgaris*). A dark-colored fish, with two small barbels and many thousands of small scales, deeply imbedded in a thick skin. In favorable light they shine with a golden, resplendent lustre. The Tench is found in muddy waters all over Europe. In Paris its scales are used to make artificial pearls. Our fishes were imported, together with the Carps, by Herr von Hessels.

126. THE SHINER. (*Notemigonus americanus*). A beautiful little fish, with a very small head, and convex dorsal and abdominal outlines. It is greenish above, brilliantly lustrous white at the sides. Length three to six inches. New England, in bayous, ponds, and weedy streams.

FAM.—*Clupeidæ*.

127. THE MOSSBONKER or MENHADEN. (*Brevoortia menhaden*). A very common fish, extensively used as manure, and as bait for Mackerel, Cod, and Halibut on the coast of Massachusetts. Its body is much compressed; the surface silvery, with a prominent humeral spot. Length ten to fourteen inches. Cape Cod to Cape Hatteras.

128. THE SHAD. (*Alosa sapidissima*). A well-known, brilliantly shining fish, of most delicate taste. Millions of it are caught all along our Eastern coast. During spawning time it ascends the larger rivers, often as far as one hundred and fifty miles.

FAM.—*Gymnotidæ*.

129. THE COMMON EEL. (*Anguilla Bostoniensis*). This species is found not only near Boston, as the name seems

to indicate, but everywhere on the coast and in the rivers of Northeast America, also in Japan, Formosa, and China. It is very variable in its colors: greenish, brownish, silvery gray, etc. Its length is from one to four feet. The eel was of great value to the Aquarium, as it afforded the principal food for the White Whales kept there.

130. THE GREEN MARAY. (*Muraena maculipinnis*). The form and habits of this fish have a great resemblance to those of a large snake. It is from three to six feet long, has a cylindrical body without pectoral fins; the dorsal and anal fins are fleshy, low, and connected with each other; the mouth is furnished with several rows of teeth, sufficiently large and sharp-pointed to inflict severe wounds. In Bermuda they catch it with a hook and line, and are very careful not to expose themselves to its bite, killing it as soon as it is caught.

The Maray is nocturnal in its habits. In day-time it generally lies motionless in a corner of its tank. When disturbed, or brought into the neighborhood of other fishes, it displays its very dangerous array of teeth. Then suddenly rushing upon its prey, it seizes and swallows it much as snakes do their food. The color of its body is green, but very dark, nearly black; the dorsal fin has a narrow white edge. It is found in tropical latitudes of the Atlantic. Our specimen was brought from Bermuda.

131. THE SPECKLED MARAY. (*Muraena moringa*). The size, form, and habits of this species are the same as of the preceding one. Its body is grayish brown, with large, irregular dots and blotches of a white or yellowish color, which give it a very handsome appearance.

In Bermuda (where we received a fine specimen), this fish is considered excellent food by the lower classes, but an impression exists that at certain seasons its flesh is poisonous. Both species are near relatives to the Maray of the Mediterranean (*Muraena helena*), made famous by the tales of ancient writers. They tell us that wealthy Romans kept these fishes in large, artificial ponds, and valued them so highly that one patrician magnate, Vedius Pollio, used to feed the flesh of his slaves to them.

ORDER LOPHOBRANCHII.

Fishes the gills of which are composed of small, rounded lobes attached to both sides of the bronchial arches. The gill opening is very small. The body is covered by a dermal skeleton consisting of numerous pieces which are arranged in segments. The joints of these pieces are generally elevated and keeled.

132. THE PIPE FISH. (*Sygnathus peckianus*). Body long and slender; the head protruding into a narrow, pipe-like snout, at the end of which the lower jaw moves like a projecting lid. When swimming, it generally keeps its body perpendicular, and moves only by handsome undulations of the long dorsal fin. The female deposits her eggs into a pouch on the tail of the male, covered by cutaneous folds. There they are kept until they develop. The newly-born young are not much thicker than a bristle. Length six to twelve inches. Newfoundland to Cape Hatteras.

133. THE SEA HORSE. (*Hippocampus hudsonius*). A very interesting little fish, with a head resembling that of a horse, and a finless, prehensile tail. As with the preceding species, the male carries the eggs and young in a sac at the base of the tail. Its swimming power is very limited, obliging it to fasten itself to seaweed or other floating substances with which it is often carried by currents to great distances. Its food consists of small crustaceans like Mysis and allied species. These it slowly approaches and suddenly sucks into its pipe-like muzzle. It will also feed on the Serpula Dianthus. Length three to six inches. Cape Cod to Cape Hatteras.

ORDER PLECTOGNATHI. FAM.—*Sclerodermi.*

134. THE EUROPEAN FILE-FISH or BERMUDA TURBOT. (*Balistes capriscus*). A large, beautiful, and remarkably shaped fish. Its body is high and compressed; its mouth very small; its skin dusky brown, and unspotted, but with obliquely-crossing lines indicating the position of the large, rough, and prominent scales. Length twelve to eighteen inches. Atlantic Ocean, on European and American coasts.

135. THE LONG-TAILED FILE-FISH. (*Alutera cuspicauda*). Body high, compressed, almost like a leaf. Skin brown, varied with orange, covered with minute asperities, making it rough like shagreen. Tail lancet-shaped, and nearly half as long as the body, the length of which is from five to eight inches. Cape Cod to Florida.

136. THE MASSACHUSETTS FILE-FISH or FOOL-FISH. (*Stephanolepis Massachusettensis*). Brown, with obscure blackish spots or streaks. Length three to seven inches. Nova Scotia to Florida.

137. THE COW-FISH. (*Ostracion quadricornis*). The appearance of this fish is very singular. The integuments of its body are modified into a three-ridged carapace composed of hexagonal, osseous scales; only the snout-like mouth, the bases of the fins, and the hind part of the tail are covered by soft skin. Over each eye there is a prominent, conical spine, pointing straight forward, and giving it the cow-like appearance. Another flat, prominent spine, directed backward, is situated on each ventral ridge. The color of the carapace is very handsome in full light, but changes a good deal. It is a

rich bright blue, with reticulated brown lines, and light ocelli. After death the color quickly vanishes.

The motions of the Cow-fish are slow and cautious. It often rests for hours at the bottom of the sea. It lives well in a large, well aërated tank, and feeds freely on shrimps and clams. Sometimes it ejects water from its mouth over the surface, to a distance of three or four feet. Its length is from twelve to twenty-one inches. Bermuda.

138. THE TRIANGULAR FISH or CUCKOLD. (*Ostracion triqueter*). Similar in shape and organization to the preceding species, but smaller, seldom exceeding eight inches, without spines, and differently colored. It is dark brown, with many yellowish-white circular spots. Its motions are livelier than those of the Cow-fish, though it is not a rapidly swimming fish. Its broad pectoral fins are constantly moving, their chief function apparently being to fan a current of water through the gills. "When taken from the water," says G. Brown Goode, "one of these fishes will live for two or three hours, all the time solemnly fanning its gills, and when restored to its native element, seems none the worse for its experiences, except that, on account of the air absorbed, it cannot at once sink to the bottom." Like the Cow-fish, it has the habit of throwing water over the surface, suddenly projecting its fleshy lips and causing a small body of water to fly through the air. West Indies and Bermuda Islands.

FAM.—*Gymnodontes*.

Fishes with a short body. The bones of the jaws instead of bearing teeth are themselves transformed into a sharp, cutting beak, the upper and lower part of which is sometimes divided by a median suture. They have no ventral fins, and the other fins are small and soft.

139. THE ROUGH PUFFER or SWELL-FISH. (*Chilichthys turgidus*). Olive green; the surface roughened with prickles; body oblong and cylindrical. This fish is abundant on our coast, and derives its name from the swollen, ball-like shape it takes when removed from the water and rubbed with the hand. It is of no value for the table. Length six to twelve inches. Cape Cod to Florida.

140. THE PORCUPINE-FISH or SEA-HEDGEHOG. (*Paradiodon hystrix*) The peculiar armor of this fish, and its

capability to swallow either air or water, thereupon assuming the form of a ball, have attracted general attention. It is abundant in the West Indies, and is found in the tropical and subtropical latitudes of other oceans. Two specimens were brought from Bermuda to the Aquarium. They were eighteen inches long, having a very thick body, a high and broad, nearly quadrangular, head, and were covered with long spines, the greater number of which were capable of being erected.

141. THE SPINY BOX-FISH or BALLOON-FISH. (*Chilomycterus geometricus*). Greenish, with numerous winding, brown stripes, and a few dark-colored blotches. The surface is covered with short, partly movable spines. This fish is able to inflate itself with water or air, taking the form of a ball in both instances. When the inflation is with water it falls to the bottom, with air it rises upside down to the surface. Length five to seven inches. Cape Cod to Cape Hatteras.

SUBCLASS GANOIDEI.

ORDER—*Holostei.*   FAM.—*Amiidæ.*

142. THE FRESHWATER DOG-FISH or MUD-FISH. (*Amia calva*). Color dark olive, with greenish markings at the sides. The male has a roundish black spot on the caudal fin; the female, which is of larger size, is without this mark. Its body is oblong and stout, the jaws are broad, rounded, and supplied with strong teeth. The dorsal fin is very long.

This fish is very interesting on account of its manner of breathing. It possesses a real lung, or rather a part of its airbladder acts as a lung. It frequently comes to the surface either to inhale or exhale air. Its respiration in this way resembles that of the proteus and of the earlier stages of frogs, toads, and salamanders, which have both lungs and gills. Its flesh is soft and pasty, but not edible. In some regions it is called "The Lawyer," because "it will bite at anything, and is good for nothing when caught."

FAM.—*Lepidosteidæ.*

143. THE GAR-PIKE. (*Lepidosteus osseus*). The body of this fish is covered with hard, enameled, lozenge-shaped,

shining plates, a peculiarity which is found in a very large proportion in the earlier fossil fishes, but which is exceedingly scarce now. Another remarkable peculiarity is, that the Gar Pike, like the preceding fish, uses part of its air-bladder as a lung, and comes to the surface to breathe.

Its body is elongated and cylindrical; its head is prolonged into a long and bony snout, exceeding in length twice the rest of the head. The color of the body is olive, with numerous black spots that are most conspicuous in the fins. Length one to five feet. It is abundant in the larger bodies of water in the North-eastern States.

ORDER—*Chondrostei.*   FAM.—*Acipenseridæ.*

Fishes with an elongated fusiform body, the skin of which is devoid of scales, but covered with five rows of bony plates. The mouth lies at the lower side of the protruding snout, is transverse, protractile, and toothless. There is a row of four barbels in front of the mouth. The tail has two unequal lobes, the upper one being the larger.

144. THE SHARP-NOSED or COMMON SEA-STURGEON. (*Acipenser sturio*). This is a handsome fish, with a very peculiar form. It has the appearance of a gallant knight, covered with a showy armor, but its habits do not agree with this appearance of valor. It lies much at the bottom, to which the heavy body, burdened by the bony shields, drag it, and there, by means of its four barbels and protractile mouth, it finds its food, which consists of vegetation and decayed animal matter. In spring it is found at the confluence of rivers where sometimes specimens of fifteen feet in length are caught. The meat, eggs (for caviar), and swimming-bladder (for isinglass) are extensively used. Atlantic Ocean, ascending rivers.

145. THE BLUNT-NOSED STURGEON. (*Acipenser brevirostris*). The snout, which in the foregoing species is pointed, and measures half the length of the head, is blunt in this one, and reaches but a quarter of the length of the head. There are 11–13 dorsal plates in A. sturio, 8–10 in A. brevirostris; 37–44 dorsal rays in the first one, 30 in the latter. Cape Cod to Florida.

SUBCLASS CHONDROPTERYGII.

ORDER—*Plagiostomata.*   FAM.—*Selachoidei.*

Fishes with an elongated and nearly fusiform body. Their skin contains an immense number of small ossifications, making it rough and shagreen-like. The pectoral fins are separated from the head (united with it in the Rays). They are easily recognized, as the elongated snout gives them a very marked appearance. The mouth, situated at the lower surface of the head, is armed with several rows of formidable teeth. There are five narrow gill-openings at each side of the neck.

This family of fishes comprises among its 125 members the largest and most dangerous of all. The majority of them are small, measuring from three to five feet, but some attain the size of thirty feet and a weight of two thousand pounds. They are the frequent companions of ocean vessels, devour whatever is thrown overboard, from the meanest article of food to man himself, don't reject even iron or wood and really take into their capacious stomach, without selection, whatever they are able to swallow. This voracious character, together with their danger to human life, creates an enmity towards them among sailors the world over. In their mutual strife it is a case of "no quarter."

146. THE BLUE SHARK. (*Eulamia Milberti*). A fish not over five feet long, which hangs around the fishermen's quarters, and feeds on offal and dead fish. It is sometimes destructive to the pounds by the force of mere numbers. Cape Cod to Florida.

147. THE SMOOTH DOG-FISH. (*Mustelus canis*). A fish of slender form, from one and a half to four feet long, in color a dull, ashy gray above, white beneath. The name is derived from the skin, which is smoother than in any other kind of shark, the ossifications being extremely small. It generally keeps near the bottom, where it feeds on crustaceans, the shell or crust of which is easily broken by their numerous and pointed teeth. It sometimes swarms in vast numbers around and into the fishermen's nets, particularly on the Massachusetts coast at Menemsha-bight. Hundreds of boys and girls are employed to take out the livers, which are used in the manufacture of fish-oil. The bodies are afterwards used as manure by the farmers. Cape Cod to Cape Hatteras.

148. THE MACKEREL SHARK. (*Isuropsis Dekayi*). A powerful fish with one very large and one small dorsal fin, and a keel on both sides of the tail. Its length is from four to eight feet. It follows the shoals of mackerel so regularly that the fishermen watch it and are guided by its movements in throwing out their nets. Newfoundland to Florida.

149. THE PICKED DOG-FISH. (*Squalus americanus*). A gray-colored Shark of one to three feet in length, with a strong spine in front of the two dorsal fins. It is the most common shark on the eastern coast of America, particularly near Newfoundland, where, in spring and autumn, it forms an important fishery for the oil which it furnishes. The fishermen avoid this shark, as it is very skillful in inflicting ugly wounds with its spines. These it dashes violently into its enemy by bending the dorsal side down and suddenly straightening it again. During nine or ten months in the year the female daily brings forth a young one six to eight inches long. The half developed eggs, which are covered by a transparent, brownish shell, can be cut out of the female and kept alive in sea-water for several days. The constantly swinging body, with the bright red external gills, and the tender blood lines which encircle the yolk and bring nourishment to the young, form a highly interesting preparation.

FAM.—*Batoidei* or *Rays*.

They resemble Sharks in their organization, but not in their external form. The body has a round or rhomboid form, the sides of which are represented by the large pectoral fins which are attached to the hind part of the head. The snout is pointed and elongated; the mouth, nostrils, and gill openings are situated at the lower, the eyes and the spiracles (small apertures behind the eyes) at the upper surface. The latter conduct new water to the gills when the rays lie at the bottom and have their mouths closed, or when they feed. The narrow and long tail generally has two dorsal and one anal fin; the latter heterocercal or unequal in its lobes. Their eyes show a very remarkable peculiarity, consisting of a fringed curtain that hangs down from the upper border of the iris and covers part of the pupil. The eggs of the Rays are wider than those of the Sharks, have a less transparent case, and resemble flat cushions, with long, coiled strings at the four corners. When deposited, the female takes the egg into her mouth and fastens it to seaweed, rocks, oyster-shells and the like.

150. THE TORPEDO, CRAMP-FISH, or NUMB-FISH. (*Torpedo occidentalis*). This fish is renowned for its electric power. The electric organs lie on both sides of the head, or between the pectoral fins and the head, and consist of numerous small boxes resembling bee-cells, which are filled with a gelatinous substance. Many tender nerves enter these boxes

from one side and, near the surface, form a complicated network of nervous cells and fibres. The side covered by the nervous network is the same in all the boxes, either the upper or the lower one, and thus an electric current is established between the two opposite sides. The surface with the network is found to be electro-positive, the other electro-negative. The electric shocks which this species can give are not dangerous, though very sharp. Fishermen are fond of making fun with it. The body of the Torpedo is a broad, smooth disk. The tail has a longitudinal fold along each side. It is found, in small numbers, from Cape Cod to Florida.

151. THE PRICKLY RAY. (*Raia americana*). Brown and unspotted, with pointed groups of prickles on the upper

surface, and four series of spines along the tail. Its length is from one to two feet. Cape Cod to Florida.

152. THE BARNDOOR SKATE. (*Raia lævis*). Light brown and unspotted, with small spines on the orbits and anterior margins of the pectoral fins. It has three rows of spines on the tail. The rest of the body is smooth, and is from two to four feet in length. Nova Scotia to Florida.

153. THE SPOTTED RAY. (*Raia ocellata*) Light brown, with numerous ocellated black spots. Its length is two to three feet. It is caught with a hook in company with the Cod. New England coasts.

154. THE STING-RAY, WHIP-RAY, or STINGAREE. (*Trygon centrura*). Above, its color is olive brown, beneath, white, tail longer than the body, and armed with two or more spines. The total length of this fish is from five to eight feet. When captured it violently whips its tail about, the spines of which can inflict ugly and dangerous wounds. Fishermen pronounce it poisonous. Cape Cod to Florida.

155. THE BUTTERFLY RAY. (*Pteroplatea maclura*). Above, the color is greenish blue, with pale spots, below, it is pale red. Its body is twice as broad as long. Its tail is very short. Its mode of swimming is very interesting, the flapping of the large sides reminding one of the motions of flying birds and butterflies. Cape Cod to Florida.

156. THE COW-NOSED RAY. (*Rhinoptera quadriloba*). This Ray differs from most of its relatives by having the head free from the pectoral fins. It is provided, however, with a pair of rayed appendages to the head called cephalic fins by some naturalists. Its tail is very slender, with a dorsal fin before the serrated spine. It is caught in the vicinity of New York, and is said to be very troublesome to the amateur fisherman, as it runs off with his bait and spoils his line. Cape Cod to Florida.

Subclass Cyclostomi.

These fishes are, with one exception, the Lancelet, the lowest and most imperfectly built of all. They have a cartilaginous skeleton, no ribs, limbs, shoulder girdle, nor pelvic elements, no real jaws, no scales, only one nostril, and their gills have the form of fixed sacs. Their mouth is nearly circular, and provided with many acute labial teeth. In their manner of feeding they resemble the leech. They fasten themselves to other fishes by suction, and feed by scraping off their flesh. The young are without teeth, have rudimentary eyes, and undergo a metamorphosis.

157. THE SEA LAMPREY. (*Petromyzon americanus*). Body olive green, mottled with dark brown; seven round gill openings on each side. Length four to six inches. Cape Cod to Cape Hatteras, ascending rivers.

158. THE SMALL LAMPREY. (*Ammocoetes appendix*). Yellowish; the seven gill openings are elongated; the anal fin has a thread-like appendix on its anterior portion. Length four to six inches. Cape Cod to Cape Hatteras, ascending rivers.

CRUSTACEA.

159. THE FIDDLER or SOLDIER CRAB. (*Gelasimus pugnax*). An amusing little crab, with one claw longer than the whole carapace. It lives in muddy banks and in ditches in salt-marshes, sometimes in such numbers that all around where they congregate it is perfectly honeycombed. When one crab goes into the hole of another a lively fight follows, and not unfrequently a general commotion takes place, after which each one gets into the first hole he can find. Cape Cod to Florida.

160. THE ROCK CRAB. (*Cancer irroratus*). Larger than the preceding, sometimes measuring three or four inches across the shell, and easily distinguished by having nine blunt teeth at the outside of each eye. It is found on rocky and sandy shores and bottoms, and is, like all the other species of crabs, greedily devoured by many of the larger fishes, such as cod, haddock, tautog, black bass, sharks, and sting-rays. Labrador to South Carolina.

161. THE MUD CRAB. (*Panopeus depressus*). A small crab, not exceeding two inches in length, with a flattened body and large, unequal claws on the two front feet. It lives on oyster-beds, and is believed to feed on the spawn of the oyster. Cape Cod to Florida.

162. THE GREEN CRAB. (*Carcinas mænas*). This crab is found in abundance on very different places along our coasts, chiefly on rocky, sandy, and muddy shores and in brackish waters. It is cosmopolitan in its habits, lives among the oysters in muddy places, or hides itself in the cavities made by fiddler-crabs in the ditches and streams of the salt marshes. Our specimens are about two inches long, and have a dark-green carapace with five teeth on the anterior margin at the outside of each eye. They are voracious and dexterous, tear the food out of the claws of large Hermit crabs, and are bold enough to put one of their large claws between the valves of different shell-fishes to pick out the soft body from the interior. Cape Cod to Florida.

163. THE LADY CRAB. (*Platyonichus ocellatus*). This is a very handsome crab, both in form and color. Its carapace is almost as wide as long. Its eyes are situated on long stalks, enabling them to protrude upward to the water when the animal is totally buried in the sand. "The Lady Crab," says Verrill, "is predaceous in its habits, feeding upon various smaller creatures, but, like most of the crabs, it is also fond of dead fishes or any other dead animals. In some localities they are so abundant that a dead fish or shark will, in a short time, be completely covered with them; but if a person should approach they will all suddenly slip off backwards and quickly disappear in every direction beneath the sand. After a short time, if everything be quiet, immense numbers of eyes and antennæ will be gradually and cautiously protruded from beneath the sand, and, after their owners have satisfied themselves that all is well, the army of crabs will soon appear above the sand again, and continue their operations."

Sometimes they are seen actively swimming near the surface of the water, their last pair of feet being flat and wide and perfectly adapted to this motion. Their ground-color is white or gray, but almost entirely covered with annular spots formed by minute red and purple specks, which give it a very handsome appearance. Its length is six inches. Cape Cod to Florida.

164. THE BLUE or EDIBLE CRAB. (*Callinectes hastatus*). Like the Lady Crab, this one has a pair of flattened legs which it can use to good purpose in swimming. The larger ones are commonly found among the eel-grass on muddy bottoms, and in brackish water. They are easily distinguished by their brilliant blue color, and by the large, sharp spine on each side of the carapace. They are caught in great numbers for the market, those having recently shed their shells, the soft-shelled crabs, being especially in demand. Cape Cod to Florida.

DECORATOR.   HORSE SHOE CRAB IN TROUBLE.

165. THE SPIDER CRAB. (*Libinia canaliculata*). This crab has a comparatively small carapace and very long legs, reminding one of the spider. The larger specimens, sometimes measuring a foot and more across the extended legs, are very sluggish in their movements, and conceal themselves in mud and decaying weeds, and hydroids, algæ, and even barnacles grow on them. The smaller specimens, when kept in a clear tank where they cannot conceal themselves, cover their back with particles of ulvæ, sponge, or whatever they can get. They pinch suitable pieces off with their claws, bring it to their mouth, cover the base of it with a kind of glue, and paste it deliberately on their back. Our tanks show several with pieces of red and gray sponge, green ulvæ and small shells, and often we are asked by visitors why we (?) had pasted on them such a mixture of ornaments. From their habits they received the by-name of "decorating spider crabs." Maine to Florida.

166. THE LONG-ARMED HERMIT CRAB. (*Eupagurus longocarpus*). This active and interesting little crab is well known to sea-side visitors from its habit of living in empty shells, in order to protect its soft hinder parts. It is very pugnacious, always ready to fight with one of its kind, but after the first encounter both retreat as far as possible into their shell and cover the aperture with the large claw. A remarkable circumstance in their organization is a lack of symmetry, or one-sidedness. Not only their claws, but the two sides of the whole

body are unequal in size, so as to fit closely in spiral shells. They are found abundantly in pools near low water, and on muddy, rocky, or sandy bottoms in deep water, where they are eagerly sought by fishes, which swallow them shell and all. Massachusetts to South Carolina.

167. THE SHORT-ARMED HERMIT CRAB. (*Eupagurus pollicaris*). This species attains a larger size, and consequently inhabits larger shells, such as pear-snails, natica, heros, etc. Its claws are shorter and thicker than those of the long-armed crab. It is devoured by sharks and sting-rays. Massachusetts to Florida.

168. THE LOBSTER. (*Homarus americanus*). It is very interesting to watch the movements of this common but strangely-shaped animal, to observe how cautiously he approaches a new inhabitant of the tank, how carefully he selects the safest corner, always ready to protect himself by his huge shears, and how suddenly he flaps his tail and glides backwards through the water. There is a handsome variety in one of the cement tanks, a lobster of a *sky-blue* color without any dark shade; another variety, entirely *scarlet*, a present of Gen. Jardine, was kept for a few days in the same tank. The latter resembled a boiled lobster, and many visitors would not believe it to be alive until they saw it moving.

These varieties show that there are two colors in the crust of a lobster, blue and red. Generally the latter is partly covered by the former, producing a color that is neither blue nor red Only in a few instances, like those of our red and blue specimens, does nature restrict itself to one color. The lobster is caught abundantly on the coast of the Northeastern States and in the Bay of Fundy.

169. THE CRAWFISH. (*Cambarus Bartonii* and allied species). This is the largest of freshwater crustaceans. It resembles the lobster, except in its size and in some minor particulars, as, for instance, the form of the last plate of the tail, which is divided, while it is entire in the lobster. American freshwater crustaceans, though numerous in species, are but scarce in number, and are seldom found in the market or known as an article of food. In Europe similar crawfishes are regularly for sale in such months as are spelled without an "r," the reverse of the rule that governs the sale of oysters.

The crawfish is remarkable for its mode of swimming. It flaps its abdomen (erroneously but usually called the tail) against its breast, and by this means swims rapidly backwards, while it uses its numerous legs for forward or lateral motion. Often it is found at a considerable distance from the streams, using occasional pools, or burrowing through a moist surface in order to reach water below. It feeds upon animal matter, both dead and alive, and is so eager for carrion that Audubon called it a "little aquatic vulture."

170. THE BLIND CRAWFISH. (*Cambarus pellucidus*). We received a few of these animals from the renowned Mammoth Cave of Kentucky. They lived for several months, being kept in a large glass globe, and though exposed to the light, there was no perceptible change in their yellowish gray color. Their eyes were seen to show externally all the peculiarities of the eye of a crawfish, having a movable peduncle, or stem, to the end of which a cornea was attached. But the microscope showed this cornea to be partly opaque and without that peculiar structure which enables an animal to get distinct optical impressions. The power of vision in these fishes is lost by disuse.

171. THE SPINY LOBSTER. (*Palinurus vulgaris*). A native of Bermuda, and distinguished from the common lobster by its red color, the spiny carapace, and the want of pincers or shears on the large legs. The same species is caught on the south-European coasts of the Atlantic and Mediterranean, sent to the market in large quantities, and is as highly appreciated as our lobster. The female carries its eggs under the abdomen, and in the same way that the crawfish and common lobster do, but the young are so different from the parent lobster, that until recently they were considered to be entirely different animals, and were described as glass shrimps, or Phyllosoma.

172. THE FLAT LOBSTER. (*Scyllarus aequinoxialis*). The body, the antennæ, and the tail plates are flat and broad; the feet are very short. This crab is very quiet, likes to bury itself out of sight, and does not live well in a tank. Its color is dark red. Length eight to twelve inches. Bermuda Islands.

173. THE SAND SHRIMP. (*Crangon vulgaris*). It is found in immense numbers on sandy flats, in tide pools, and on the sandy bottoms in deeper water. Numerous fishes

feed on it, such as the weak-fish, king-fish, blue-fish, flounder, striped bass, sea-robin, toad-fish, etc. If it were not such a prolific species it might be extinguished in a short time. In dangerous places it buries itself partially in the sand. The appearance of the sand shrimp in a tank with clear water plainly shows how the beauty of an animal and the interest it inspires depends upon its being seen in natural condition. He who knows the shrimp only as he sees it in the market-basket, will hardly believe that the handsome, transparent creature with beautiful caudal plates is naught but the little, dark gray mass of salted morsel with an ugly agglomeration of crooked legs he used to know under this name. It is found on both sides of the northern Atlantic Ocean.

174. THE SILVER-SHRIMP. (*Pandanus annulicornis*). Sold for fish-bait in the New York markets. It lives well in the tanks, is useful as a scavenger and as food for nearly all fishes. Northern Atlantic.

175. THE COMMON PRAWN. (*Palæmonetes vulgaris*). Similar to the former, but easily distinguished by its bigger body and by the possession of a denticulated spine at the front. It is found in countless numbers among the eel-grass in brackish waters, and on many other places from Massachusetts to the Carolinas. For the table it is preferred to the shrimp.

176. THE LOCUST-CRAB. (*Squilla empusa*). This is a very peculiar and interesting creature, living on muddy bottoms, and probably burrowing out of sight for the larger part of the year. It is sometimes caught in considerable numbers among the ice at the mouth of the Hudson. Its length, when full grown, is eight or ten inches. In our tanks they swim very lively during day-time, bend their body to a half circle, move their numerous feet incessantly with astonishing rapidity, and feed during the night. Cape Cod to Florida.

177. IDOTEA CÆCA. Lives parasitic on fishes, and was taken off in great numbers from drum-fishes, striped bass, and others. Massachusetts to Florida.

178. LIVONECA OVALIS. Taken off the gills of striped bass.

179. LERNEOLEMA RADIATA. Parasitic on moss-bonkers, striped bass, and other fishes.

180. THE BARNACLE. (*Balanus balanoides*). This animal resembles a low, blunt cone fastened to stones or shells. Periodically a small, hardly perceptible bunch of fine threads is thrown out from the upper end and quickly drawn back again. These threads, which are twenty-four in number, are the divided and minutely articulated legs of which the barnacle has six on each side. By their movements it draws water and food into its shell. The young are quite different from the old ones, and are able to swim. After fastening themselves they not only lose the ability to swim, but also the eye, and thus constitute an example of retrograde metamorphosis through which the individual loses and the species gains, as the power of reproduction inheres in the Barnacle only in its advanced condition of life.

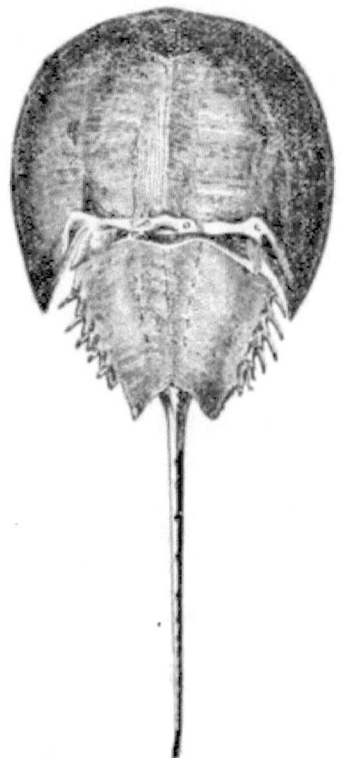

THE HORSE-SHOE CRAB.

181. THE GOOSE-BARNACLE. (*Lepas fascicularis*). Found in Wood's Hole on floating timber. Lived a short time in the tanks.

182. THE HORSE-SHOE CRAB or KING-CRAB. (*Limulus polyphemus*). Common on sandy shores, just below water-mark; more abundant still on muddy bottoms, where it buries just beneath the surface and feeds upon various small animals. The upper side of this large crab at first sight shows nothing but two large shields and a long spine, the lower shield exhibiting a complicated agglomeration of legs. Looking closer, two large eyes are found on the front shield, and two smaller eyes are lying in front of them. The mouth, situated at the lower surface, is surrounded by six pairs of differently shaped legs, the claws of which are employed to seize the food and conduct it to their own basal parts in order to be crushed and lacerated by them. The same organs combine the triple function of moving, seizing the food, and preparing it for digestion. The hinder part of the lower side carries another dozen of legs, which also have a double function. They act as swimming organs, and at the same time cause a current of water to flow to the gills.

The usual motion of the King-crab is slow crawling; their swimming is awkward, and easily interrupted by trivial causes. This accounts for the frequency with which they are found struggling on their backs. Their spawning season is in June and July. They are found from Maine to Florida.

ANNELIDA.

183. LEPIDONOTUS SUBLEVIS. Found at Martha's Vineyard. It lives well in a tank, but hides away out of sight.

184. THE SANDWORM. (*Nereis pelagica*). Sold in the market as fish-bait. In the tanks it buries out of sight, feeds at night, and is very destructive to Algæ.

185. POTAMILLA OCULIFERA. Attached to scollop-shells.

186. EUCHONE ELEGANS. A beautiful creature, introduced in our tanks from Wood's Hole.

187. THE CLINKER. (*Serpula dianthus*). Worms which surround themselves with a calcareous, variously crooked tube, and live in colonies on stones and shells. Generally their red, comb-like gills protrude from the opening of the tube, but they quickly draw them back and close the tube with a hard, purplish cover when they are frightened by a knock at the glass, or otherwise disturbed. They are found from Cape Cod to Great Egg Harbor.

Mollusca.

188. THE EIGHT-FOOTED POLYP or DEVIL-FISH. (*Octopus vulgaris*). We received several of these very interesting animals from Bermuda, but they all died after being only a few days in the tanks.

Their body consists of a large bag, a small head with two big eyes, and eight long arms connected with each other by an intermediate skin at their base. They breathe by taking the water through a wide opening at the base of the bag into two large gills, and ejecting it again through a short and thick siphon. The latter current at the same time serves as the moving power of the animal.

One specially attractive feature of the Devil-fish is the possession of several hundreds of sucking disks distributed in two rows on each arm. Each disk is a short, thick cylinder, the center of which can be raised so as to establish a vacuum between itself and the part to which it adheres. The sucking power of a medium-sized Devil-fish, one of about three feet in length, is large enough to enable it to move stones of forty pounds weight. As the weight of a man in water is about five pounds, it would be no difficulty for a large Octopus to drag him under water. The food of the Octopus consists of shells, crustaceans, and occasionally fishes. It surrounds and covers its prey with its arms so completely as to prevent even a large-sized, healthy lobster from using its powerful claws.

189. THE GIANT DEVIL-FISH. (*Architeuthis princeps*). We take leave to insert in this place the following very interesting letter of Prof. A. E. Verrill, the naturalist who discovered this species:

PEABODY MUSEUM OF YALE COLLEGE,
NEW HAVEN, CONN., *Oct.* 11, 1877.

MESSRS. CHAS. REICHE & BROTHER,
NEW YORK AQUARIUM.

GENTLEMEN :—Thanks to your courtesy, I yesterday had an opportunity to examine the "giant squid" or "devil fish" now preserved in the New York Aquarium, and to make careful measurements of its parts. Having made a special study of these remarkable animals during several years past, and having previously examined and described all the fragments of similar creatures preserved in the museums of this country, I am able to say that this is altogether *the largest, most complete, and most valuable specimen of this kind that has ever been preserved either in this country or in Europe.* Moreover, it is a very rare species, previously known to scientific men only by the jaws taken from the stomach of a sperm whale, which were first described and figured by me three years ago under the name of *Architeuthis princeps*. When first captured your specimen was carefully measured by my correspondent, the Rev M. Harvey, of St. Johns, Newfoundland, who, in a private letter, states that the body was 9½ feet long including the head, and the longest arms were 30 feet in length, making the total length 39½ feet. The circumference of the body was seven feet. In preserving creatures of this kind, either in brine or alcohol, they always shrink very much in bulk and lose most of their natural color and form. Your specimen having been brought to New York in brine, and since its arrival having been kept in strong alcohol, has necessarily contracted considerable in size already, and will probably shrink still more after some weeks. The body, originally plump and round, has also collapsed and become flat. I yesterday found that the long arms are now 24 feet and 1 inch long, with the broader terminal portion bearing the suckers 3 feet in length and 3 inches in breadth ; the larger suckers, now mostly destroyed, were about an inch in diameter. These suckers, with many smaller ones along the borders and at the end of the arms, were provided with strong, bony rims with the edge cut into numerous sharp teeth to prevent the suckers from slipping when applied to the slippery skin of the fishes upon which they prey. Below these serrated suckers, and extending along the inner surface of the arms for sixteen feet, there are many small suckers, with smooth rims, together with wart-like tubercles which fit into the suckers of the opposite arms. These are intended to fasten the two long arms securely together so that they can be used conjointly and thus more effectually secure large prey.

The longest of the eight stouter arms around the mouth were originally 11 feet long and 17 inches in circumference at the base, tapering gradually to the tips. I found them 10½ feet long and 11½ inches in circumference. These arms are all covered, along their inner surface, with large suckers arranged in two rows, and provided with sharp-toothed rims, the largest being an inch in diameter. The jaws form a large and powerful black beak, shaped like a parrot's, and capable of being protruded beyond the head when living. With this beak they doubtless instantly kill their prey when caught by biting out a piece from the back of the neck, thus severing the spinal cord, as their relatives, the small squids, are known to do. The upper jaw, measured by me, was 5¼ inches long, and 3 and 3⅛ broad; the lower jaw was 3¾ inches long and 3¼ broad. The upper jaw shuts into the lower, unlike the beaks of birds. It is practically impossible to obtain these giant squids in a perfect condition, for they are very shy and very tenacious of life, and living entirely in deep water, they are seldom or never seen unless disabled.

There is but one solitary instance on record of a specimen in good health being captured, and that was very badly mutilated by the fishermen before they could take it from the rocks in which it had accidentally become entangled. That one was considerably smaller than your specimen, and is now, in part, preserved in the Peabody Museum of Yale College, but its body was entirely destroyed. Most of the few specimens hitherto seen have, like your example, been found cast upon the remote shores of Newfoundland after severe gales, and are generally badly damaged when found.

Very respectfully yours,
A. E. VERRILL,
Professor of Zoology in Yale College.

---

190. THE WHELK. (*Buccinum undatum*). Dredged at Georgias Bank, Mass., in forty fathoms. It did not live well in the tanks. The shells are favorites of the Hermit-crabs.

191. THE WINKLE. (*Sycotypus canaliculatus*). This is one of the largest shells on the eastern coast of North America, sometimes measuring seven inches in length. It is pear-shaped, and has a wide opening which continues in a narrow channel. Its eggs are contained in membranous cases of about the size and thickness of a two-cent piece, united together in a parallel position by a ligamentous string about two feet in length. Each case contains about two hundred eggs, but only a few of them develop young ones, which, when brought out, in the first weeks of their existence, feed upon the immatured eggs of the same case. It is astonishing that one snail is able to produce such an enormous quantity of eggs and cases, the bodily mass of which seems to be greater than the body of the snail itself. It is found from Cape Cod to Florida.

192. THE LARGE WINKLE. (*Fulgur carica*). This is, according to Binney, the largest convoluted shell on the Atlantic coast. It is found in company with the preceding species, but less abundantly. Its form is nearly the same, but it can easily be distinguished by a circular series of triangular, compressed tubercles just above the opening. The strings of egg-cases resemble those of the former, and are produced by the females while they are buried a few inches below the surface of the sand between tide-marks. Fishermen when tarring the seams of their boats, fill a Fulgur with hot tar and use the spout-like end of the shell to direct the flow of the tar. Hence the local name of *ladle-shell.* The animals are eaten in large quantities by negro fishermen back of Keyport, N. J., which locality has been named Winkletown, from the fact that in front of each cabin there are large accumulations of empty winkle-shells. It is found from Cape Cod to Florida.

193. THE LITTLE WHELK. (*Ilyanassa obsoleta*). Lives in great numbers on our neighboring coasts and is very useful as a scavenger. It deposits its egg-capsules freely on the glass, but they never mature there. Hydractinia polyclina often covers the shells, which are also the favorites of the small Hermit-crabs.

194. THE OYSTER-DRILL. (*Urosalpinx cinerea*). Next to the starfish this shell is the greatest enemy to young oysters and clams. It drills a minute hole near the hinge and then sucks the animal out. Common on our coast.

195. EUPLEURA CAUDATA. Dredged at Wood's Hole. Lives well in the tanks.

196. THE COMMON PURPLE. (*Purpura lapillus*). Found in Buzzard's Bay, Mass., on rocks between tide-marks, feeding on barnacles. This shell contains, inside its mantle, a yellowish-white band, of which a beautiful color is manufactured. When exposed to the sun, it quickly gets yellow, then green, blue, and at last bluish red. It is one of the shells which furnished the celebrated Tyrian purple of the ancients.

197. THE NAVEL-SHELL. (*Neverita duplicata*). The Hermit-crabs prefer the empty Navel-shells to all others. The beautiful flooded sand-cups cast ashore on Coney Island in the summer season are the egg-receptacles of this shell; the fishermen call them mermaid-collars. When placed under a magnifying-glass thousands of young shells may be seen in their sand-bound cells, propelled by their rapidly moving cilia. Many of these egg-receptacles have been exhibited in the tanks. Massachusetts Bay to Florida.

198. THE JINGLE-SHELL. (*Anomia glabra*). Attached to oysters, scollops, and other shell-fish. They are resplendent with a golden or silvery lustre.

199. THE BOAT-SHELL. (*Crepidula fornicata*). This small shell is found on other dead shells inhabited by Hermit-crabs, or on oysters, scollops, or winkles. Sometimes dozens of them adhere together, and those lowest in the group cling to other animals, empty shells, or pebbles. Their form resembles that of a trough or boat half covered by a straight piece. It grows an inch in length, and is found in great numbers on gravelly bottoms from Massachusetts to Florida.

200. THE PILL-BUG SHELL. (*Chætopleura apiculata*). The shell of this snail is composed of eight movable plates, and has the form of a trough. It is found adhering to stones and dead shells, and generally chooses its place so well that the surroundings are uniform with its colors, thereby avoiding detection. When detached from its base it either moves with considerable rapidity through the water, or curls itself into a ball like a "pill-bug" (*Oniscus*), or like an Armadillo. Its length is six to nine inches. Cape Cod to Florida.

201. MONTAGUA PILATA. This beautiful mollusk was introduced into the tanks on masses of tube-flowers, together

with clusters of Vorticellæ, on which it fed. At times it may be seen moving about freely on the glass. Massachusetts Bay to Long Island Sound.

202. THE SOFT-SHELLED or LONG CLAM. (*Mya arenaria*). Used extensively as food north of New York. It is very interesting to see the long, siphon-tubes stretched out, sometimes to the length of a foot or more. They easily bury by means of it to a considerable depth beneath the sand. South Carolina to the Arctic Ocean.

203. CORBULA CONTRACTA. Found in Gravesend Bay and Gowanus Bay, L. I., attached to muscles and tube-flowers.

204. CLIDIOPHORA TRILINEATA. Dredged at Gay Head, Mass. It lives well in a tank.

205. THE RAZOR-FISH or KNIFE-HANDLE. (*Ensatella americana*). This fish inhabits a very long and narrow shell, the front and back of which is parallel and slightly curved, the surface smooth and yellowish-green. The animal itself is still longer than the shell, so that the foot projects on one end, the two short siphons on the other. It is found on a sandy bottom where the water is clear. There it constructs a burrow of two or three feet deep, and rests at the upper end of it, keeping the orifices of the siphons in water. Sometimes, owing to the tide, it is left behind, projecting one or two inches above the ground. If cautiously approached it then may safely be drawn out with a sudden jerk, but once out of sight it is safe from capture, being able to penetrate the sand quicker than it can be followed. Its length is from four to six inches. Labrador to Florida.

206. THE SEA-, SURF- or SKIMMER-CLAM. (*Mactra solidissima*). This is a very large shell, sometimes more than six inches long and four or five inches broad. The smaller ones are well-flavored and extensively used for the dinner table. It got the name of Skimmer-clam from the Dutch settlers, who used to skim the milk with their shells. It lives on sandy shores, below low-water mark, from Labrador to North Carolina.

207. THE ROUND, HARD or QUAHOG-CLAM. (*Venus mercenaria*). Found in enormous quantities on sandy shores, but chiefly on sandy and muddy flats, just beyond low-water mark. Millions of them are sold in the markets, mostly coming

from muddy estuaries and having a rough, thick, dull-white, or mud-stained shell; those from sandy shores are thinner, more delicate, often with high, thin ribs, especially when young; some varieties are handsomely marked with angular, or zigzag lines or streaks of red or brown (*var. notata*). They are well adapted to bury, having a large, muscular foot with a broad, thin edge that can be moved at any part of the ventral side. Massachusetts Bay to Florida.

208. THE IRISH CUAHOG. (*Argina pexata*). Dredged at Tarpaulin Cove, Mass. It is a beautiful shell with bright red gills and mantle.

209. THE COMMON MUSCLE. (*Mytilus edulis*). Common on all neighboring coasts and sold in the New York and Boston markets. It is found attached by means of byssusthreads to timber and rocks. In the Baltic Ocean and on the French coasts it is extensively cultivated.

210. MODIOLA MODIOLUS. A handsome muscle, dredged at Wood's Hole, Mass. It has the habit of putting out its foot and reaching fragments of stones and algæ to attach itself.

211. MODIOLA PLICATULA. Found in neighboring creeks in brackish water. It lives well in a tank.

212. MODIOLARIA NIGRA. A large, showy muscle, dredged at Cape Cod. The Sea-squirts live on them.

THE DANCING SCOLLOPS.

213. THE SCOLLOP. (*Pecten irradians*). The shell is orbicular, with an angular appendage for the hinge, and about twenty rounded ribs, which give it a comb-like appearance. Its color is varying, mostly dusky horn, with white, yellowish, or reddish bands, very pleasing to the eye, and making the shell of use for ornamental purposes.

A peculiar feature of the Scollop is its dancing movement when alarmed. This is performed by opening and energetically closing its valves; and continuing these movements, and thus periodically expelling the water from the gill-cavity, it is sent upwards or along the surface of the water. When it rests in safety, it sends out two rows of numerous, tapering papillæ, or tentacles, and between them there may be observed a number of handsome, bright silvery, or bluish eyes, sparkling with a brilliancy equal to the brightest jewels. The Scollop is found in abundance in many localities, particularly in sheltered, muddy places, from Cape Cod to Florida. The large and powerful central muscle is sold in the markets, and considered by many persons as an excellent article of food.

Tunicata.

214. MOLGULA MANHATTENSIS. Found in Gravesend Bay attached to ulva. It lives well in confinement, even in self-supporting tanks.

215. BOTRYLLUS GOULDII. A beautiful and interesting creature, found in Gravesend Bay, growing on Zostera marina. It lives well in confinement.

Echinodermata.

216. STRONGYLOCENTROTUS DRÖBACHIENSIS. Common in deep water; does not live well in a tank.

217. THE PURPLE SEA-URCHIN. (*Arbacia punctulata*). A small species with rather stout and long purplish spines placed upon a hard, rounded shell composed of many plates. It moves, like a star-fish, by suckers which protrude through small holes in the shell. The mouth, situated in the center of the lower side, has five very large, hard teeth connected with a peculiar organ resembling a fancy lantern called the lantern of Aristotle. It feeds upon vegetables, such as diatoms and other small algæ; but is also fond of dead fishes, which it devours bones and all. It is found from Vineyard Sound to the West Indies.

218. THE SAND DOLLAR. (*Echinarachnius parma*).
Found on sandy bottoms around Long Island. It lived a short
time in our tanks.

219. THE GREEN STAR-FISH. (*Asterias arenicola*).
As in most of the other Echinoderms the different parts of its
body are repeated five times. It has five arms, and five times
four rows of sucking-feet in their inferior furrows. It has five
eyes, situated at the tips of the arms. Its nervous system consists of five longitudinal strings, connected in a ring round the
central mouth, and there are five lines of blood-vessels, and an
equal number of intestines and ovaries.

This Star-fish is found in large numbers among the rocks at
the bottom of the sea, especially where shell-fish, on which it
feeds, are abundant. It is very destructive to oyster-beds,
clinging to the oyster with its suckers somewhat after the man-

ner of the Octopus. Its mode of eating is singular. Covering the soft parts of whatever is selected for its food, it turns the digestive sac inside out, and proceeds at leisure to suck the animal from its shell. The color of this species is dark brownish green, with a small orange disk near the center of the upper side. Its diameter is about five inches. It is found from Massachusetts Bay to Florida.

220. THE GIGANTIC STAR-FISH. (*Oreaster gigas*). A large and splendid animal. Its orange-colored body is high in the center, and its surface is covered with prominent warts. Further, there are numerous small pores, through which short, slender, transparent tubes stick out, acting as respiratory organs. Our specimens came from Florida.

ACALEPHÆ.

221. THE TUBE-FLOWERS. (*Eudendrium dispar and ramosum*). These are colonies of little polyps of a plant-like appearance. The individuals occupy the ends of the branches. When examined closely with a magnifying-glass, they are found to possess two circles of slender, transparent tentacles. By means of poisonous lasso-cells they kill small animals, take them into a cavity below the center of the tentacles, and send the nutritious matter through the whole colony. Sometimes small buds are seen at the base of the exterior tentacles; these are young ones, who soon detach themselves, swim around a short while, and at last settle on stones to give origin to new colonies.

POLYPS or ANTHOZOA.

Cylindrical animals with an opening (the mouth) in the center of the upper end. This mouth is surrounded by six, eight, or many more hollow tentacles which are used to seize the food. As soon as the food reaches the mouth, it is pressed down into a central, longitudinal bag, or tube (the stomach), where it is retained and digested. This having been completed the nutritious matter passes through the lower, open end of the stomach into the cavity of the body and thence upwards into the space between the walls of the stomach and body. This space is divided by radiating partitions into many longitudinal sections or tubes, which continue into the hollow of one or several tentacles. The nutritious matter can, as it will easily be understood, reach the summit of every tentacle.

The Polyps either live singly or in colonies, in which latter case they form the coral reefs. The former are larger, but both display a wondrous beauty of form and color.

THE FRINGED SEA-ANEMONE.

222. THE FRINGED SEA-ANEMONE. (*Metridium marginatum*). This is the most common among the Polyps of North America. It is easily distinguished by the soft, plumy, tentacular fringes that surround the disk. When contracted, it looks like a mere lump of brownish or whitish jelly, but when expanded and erect it shows such grace and beauty as to attract general attention. "From the extended base," says Prof. Verrill, "the body rises in the form of a tall, smooth column, sometimes cylindrical, sometimes tapering slightly to the middle, and then enlarging to the summit. Toward the top the column is surrounded by a circular, thickened fold, above which the character of the surface suddenly changes, the skin becoming thinner and translucent, so that the internal radiating partitions are visible through it. This part expands upward and outward to the margin, which is folded into numerous deep undulations or frills, and everywhere covered with very numerous, fine, short, crowded tentacles." Its color varies from pure white through yellow, orange, and pink to dark brown.

When a Sea-anemone slowly glides along the surface of a rock or glass wall, it often leaves small particles of its body behind. These generally assume the form of warts, and in about eight days send out very thin and transparent tentacles. Besides this manner of reproduction the Sea-anemone propagates by division or through eggs.

223. THE WHITE-ARMED ANEMONE. (*Sagartia leucolena*). A small species, with a slender, pale flesh-colored, translucent, and usually whitish body, with numerous tentacles. Cape Cod to North Carolina.

224. THE STOUT-ARMED ANIMAL FLOWER. (*Tælia crassicornis*). This is the largest and brightest of the North American Polyps. It is found also on the European coasts. Its body and disk (the flat upper end of the animal) is beautifully marked with red or brown stripes, between which the stout tentacles arise. It feeds on muscles and small fishes, and sometimes attacks animals which are too vigorous to remain its victim. If the body suddenly contracts, the water is ejected through small openings at the tip of its tentacles. Sometimes a white, folded skin is seen on top of its disk; this is the stomach thrown out in order to be emptied and cleaned.

225. THE BERMUDA ANEMONES. There are three species of them in the Aquarium not yet identified. One of

them is small, and dark purplish red; the second has a grayish white body covered with red warts, the tentacles being light colored with red tips; the third is translucent so as to show the internal, radiating partitions very clearly, and has short tentacles forming a beautiful fringe around the large disk.

226. THE NEW ENGLAND CORAL. (*Astrangia Danæ*). This in the only true coral yet discovered on the coast of New England. Its colonies, which are found clinging to little fragments of rocks in sheltered creeks and inlets, consist of a small number of comparatively large individuals, each about two-thirds of an inch in height. They are whitish and translucent; their tentacles are thickly covered with small warts consisting of clusters of lasso-cells. The interior of a lasso-cell consists of a kind of poisonous fluid and a long, coiled-up bristle, which darts out and, with its numerous sharp points and hooks, fastens itself to such small worms or crustaceans as are within reach. The lime secreted by them is only found at the base of the animal, and consists of a disk. with interior, radiating, low walls, the production of the fleshy base and partitions.

Sponges.

227. THE RED SPONGE. (*Microciona prolifera*). A beautiful, dark red, or orange red species, which, when young, incrusts the surface of stones and shells, but at a later period rises to irregular lobes with many repeatedly divided, slender branches. It consists of stout horny fibres radiating from the center to the periphery, and terminating in irregular papillæ, which are the bearers of spiculæ. Cape Cod to South Carolina.

WEBER
GRAND SQUARE AND UPRIGHT
PIANO FORTE.

Hear what the Great Artists and Musicians say of them.

NILSSON. I shall take every opportunity to RECOMMEND and PRAISE your instruments.

KELLOGG. For the last six years your Pianos have been my CHOICE for the CONCERT ROOM and my own HOUSE.

PATTI. I have used the Pianos of every celebrated maker, but GIVE YOURS THE PREFERENCE OVER ALL.

CARY. I feel that every one is FORTUNATE who owns a Weber Piano, because of its rich and sympathetic quality of tone.

LUCCA. Your Uprights are EXTRAORDINARY instruments, and deserve their GREAT SUCCESS.

MURSKA. Your instruments surpass my expectations, and I rank you JUSTLY AS THE FOREMOST MANUFACTURER OF THE DAY.

CARRENO. I am not surprised that every great artist prefers the Weber Pianos; they are truly "noble" instruments, and "meet every requirement of the most exacting artist."

STRAUSS. Your Pianos astonish me; I assure you that I HAVE NEVER yet seen ANY PIANOS WHICH EQUAL YOURS.

CAMPANINI. The Weber Pianos SUSTAIN the voice in a WONDERFUL DEGREE, and they have my unqualified admiration.

WEHLI. Mme. **Parepa** called your Pianos the finest in the United States. I "fully endorse" that opinion. They have no "rival anywhere."

MILLS. Amongst the many excellent Pianos made in the city, THE WEBER RANKS FOREMOST.

MUZIO. I consider the Weber Pianos THE BEST PIANOS IN THE WORLD.

BRISTOW. To me the Weber Piano contains every thing that can be wished for in an instrument.

WAREROOMS,
Fifth Avenue and Sixteenth Street.

INDEX.

	NO.		NO.
ALLIGATOR	17	Dolphin	4
Anemonæ	220-223	Drum-fish	64
Angel-fish	53-55		
" Long Island	74	EEL	129
Angler	79	Eel-pout	83
Architeuthis	189	Euchore	186
Axolotl	23	Eupleura	195
BALLOON-FISH	141	FILE-FISH	135-136
Barnacle	180	Fishing-frog	79
Bass, Black Fresh-water	41	Flasher	47
" Black Sea	34	Flounder	99
" Fresh-water	40	Flying Robin	63
" Red	67	Four-eyed fish	52
" Striped	32	Frog, horned	18
Bellows-fish	79		
Bergall	90	GAR-PIKE	143
Black-fish	89	Ghost-fish	82
Blind-fish	115	Glass-snake	19
Blow-fish	139	Gold-fish	119
Blue-fish	76	Goose Barnacle	181
Boat-shell	199	Goose-fish	79
Botryllus	215	Gourami	85
		Grouper	35
CARP	118	Grunt	43-45
Cat-fishes	102-105	Gurnard	61-62
Chubsucker	117		
Clam	202, 206, 207	HADDOCK	94
Clidiophora	204	Hamlet	35
Clinker	187	Harvest-fish	71
Cod-fish	92	Hellbender	24
Codling	96, 97	Hermit-crab	166, 167
Conger-eel	83	Hind	36
Coral	224	Hippopotamus	1
Corbula	203	Hog-fish	88
Coui	8	Horse-crevallé	72
Cow-fish	137	Horse-fish	75
Cow-pilot	87	Horse-shoe Crab	182
Crabs	159-167		
Cramp-fish	150	IDOTEA	177
Craw-fish	169, 170		
Cuahog, Irish	208	JINGLE-SHELL	198
Cuckold	138		
Cunner	90	KILLI-FISH	65
		King-crab	182
DACE	112-114	King-fish	65
Devil-fish	188, 189	Kingiyo	120
Doctor-fish	84		
Dog-fish, Fresh-water	142	LAFAYETTE-FISH	66
" picked	149	Lamper-eel	83
" smooth	147	Lamprey	157, 158
Dollar-fish	71	Lepidonotis	183

(81)

INDEX.

	NO.
Lerneolema	179
Livoneca	178
Lobster	163
" flat	172
" spiny	171
Locust-crab	176
Maray	130, 131
Margate-fish	46
Modiola	210, 211
Modiolaria	212
Molgula	214
Monkey-fish	75
Monk-fish	79
Montagua	201
Moor-fish	56
Mossbonker	127
Mud Puppy	26
Mullet	86
Muscle	209
Muskallunge	110
Navel-shell	197
Nereis	184
Octopus	188
Oyster-drill	194
Perch	31
Pickerel	111
Pike	109–112
" Wall-eyed	33
Pill-bug shell	200
Pilot-fish	69
Pipe-fish	132
Pollock	95
Porcupine-fish	140
Porgee	50, 51
Potamilla	185
Prawn	175
Proteus	23, 26
Puffer	139
Purple	196
Ray	150–156
Razor-fish	205
Remora	70
River-horse	1
Roach	123
Rock-fish	37
Rudder-fish	77
Rusty Dab	100
Salamander	20–22
Salmon	103
Sand-dollar	218
Sargo	50
Scheltopusik	19
Scollop	213

	NO.
Sculpin	57–59
Sea-devil	79
Sea-horse	133
Sea-raven	57
Sea-robin	61
Sea-urchin	216–218
Sea-wolf	81
Seal	2, 3
Sergeant-major	87
Serpula	187
Shad	128
Shark	146–149
Sheepshead	49
Sheepshead Lebias	113
Shiner	126
Shrimp	173–175
Silver-bream	48
Skate	150–156
Slippery Dick	91
Snapper	39
Sole	101
Sponge	225
Squeteague	68
Squirrel	30
Star-fish	219, 220
Stickleback	27–29
Stink-pot	18
Strongylocentrus	216
Stumpfoot	19
Sturgeon	144, 145
Sucker	116
Sucker-fish	70
Sun-fish	42
Tautog	89
Telescopic-fish	121
Tench	125
Terrapin	11
Thread-fish	74
Toad-fish	78
Tom-cod	93
Tortoise	7–14
Triangular Fish	138
Triple-tail	47
Trout	106, 107
Turbot, Bermuda	134
" spotted	93
Tube-flower	219
Turtle	12–16
Walking-fish	80
Weak-fish	68
Whelk	190, 193
White Whale	6
Winkle	191, 192
Wry-mouth	82
Yellow Mackerel	73
Yellow-tail	38

Publisher's Department.

THE AQUARIUM GUIDE.

The Publishers of the AQUARIUM GUIDE take pleasure in calling the attention of its thousands of readers to the announcements contained in this department. Messrs. Chas. Reiche & Bro., the proprietors of the New York Aquarium, with the efficient aid of Dr. Dorner, and the assistance of many artists, have made the Guide book not only invaluable to every visitor to the Great New York Aquarium, but of such permanent value as to make it of lasting interest to every lover of nature.

It is the purpose of the Publishers to have this department in keeping with the whole book.

Only approved advertisements will be admitted, and the representations concerning advertisers may be relied upon as being strictly truthful.

The Publishers thus hope to realize their aim, which is to make this department of the AQUARIUM GUIDE of real service to the many thousands whom they are privileged to address.

CONTRIBUTORS.

Every advertiser may be regarded as a contributor whose "article" will be worthy of careful attention. Among these contributors are many of the best business concerns in New York.

ATTENTION

Will inevitably be attracted to what the following houses have to say to our readers.

TIFFANY & CO.

For elegance in design, beauty of workmanship, and fineness in quality, the goods of this famous house have a world wide reputation. What they have to say on page 8 will interest our readers.

WEBER PIANOS.

After what has been said by the famous artists quoted on page 80, in praise of these instruments, we can only recommend purchasers to profit by their judgment and experience.

Brown's "Perfect" Letter File,

Self-Indexing and Self-Binding, is undoubtedly the simplest and best thing of the kind, and the only one suitable for library use or private correspondence. The trade supplied by D. I. Carson & Co., 100 Nassau Street.

THE TEACHER'S BIBLE.

We know the purchaser of one of these elegant Bibles will never be disappointed in any respect.

They are all they are represented to be. See page 90.

PLATE GLASS

Should be bought of thoroughly reliable houses, such as the one set forth on page 89. The fact that they are patronized by the proprietors of the Aquarium is a strong recommendation.

CHROMATIC CRYSTAL SIGNS.

These are emphatically and literally "signs of the times," and are a necessity to every business man.

Messrs. D. I. Carson will furnish them in every variety, as announced on page 85.

G. GUNTHER.

The name of Gunther has long been associated with the manufacture of bird cages. His display of stock in this line is worthy of inspection. Advertisement on page 6.

W. H. BROWNING.

We would call the attention of contractors and builders to the advertisement of W. H. Browning on page 5.

W. H. GIFFING.

Torry Bros., the well known poster, show bill and general printers, have been succeeded by Mr. W. H. Giffing, whose advertisement will be found on page 88.

SIEBRECHT & WADLEY.

All lovers of flowers (and we take it for granted that means every visitor to the Aquarium) should take their earliest opportunity to visit the splendid floral establishment advertised on page 1.

MUNN & CO.

The advertisement of the long established house of Munn & Co., Publishers of the Scientific American, will be found on page 87.

E. REMINGTON & SONS.

Remington's guns helped Osman Pasha to make his brave stand against the Russians. The guns advertised on page 1 will be found — in their place — equally serviceable.

PHOTO-ELECTROTYPE CO.

Process Engraving has lately been brought to great perfection, and the above Company shows some excellent specimens of work, at greatly reduced prices. See page 2.

REICHE & BRO.

One of the most enterprising and famous establishments of its kind in the United States, the house of Rieche & Bro. The whole world is tributary to their immense business; and the record of their various transactions would read like romance. The Great New York Aquarium is but one of their great enterprises. Information regarding others will be found on last page of cover.

B. GREENWOOD.

Many of the visitors to the Acquarium will desire to adorn their homes with private aquaria. Everything necessary to this end may be found at Greenwood's Advertisement page 3.

ROSSITUR & SKIDMORE.

"At once delicate and substantial" is the verdict regarding the prepared meats offered by this enterprising house. We have tried them, and know whereof we affirm. Advertisement second page of cover.

Osborn Manufacturing Co.

As an example of what can be accomplished by good business talent, combined with courteous and fair dealing, this concern may serve as a model to younger houses. Their delightful bird cages, which have received high awards, are advertised on page 4.

WILKINS.

"A bijou bird paradise," is a fit term with which to describe the aviary of Wilkins. It is worthy of a visit, and is very near the Aquarium. See page 90.

D. I. CARSON & CO.

Book buyers, authors, and those who desire to have printing, engraving, &c., done in a satisfactory manner, or who wish to make purchases in the line of stationer's goods should read the advertisement on third page of cover.

Chromatic Crystal Signs

ELEGANCE! ECONOMY!

D. I. CARSON & CO., 100 NASSAU STREET,

NEW YORK.

Are Manufacturers' Agents for the above goods, and would call especial attention to their unrivalled facilities for supplying

LIGHT AND ELEGANT SIGNS

FOR

STORES,
    SHOW WINDOWS,
        PHYSICIANS,
            DENTISTS,
                LAWYERS,
                      NOTARIES, &c.

These signs are made in every conceivable variety, from plain Gold on Plate Glass to most ornate and artistic combinations in colors, and are the MOST PERFECT THING OF THE KIND EVER MADE.

A WORD OF ADVICE.

These Signs, unlike those painted on windows and doors, *can be removed*, and are *far more attractive*.

To secure them is to SAVE MONEY.

Send for Prices.

D. I. CARSON & CO.,
100 Nassau Street.

THE

Aquarium is Lighted

BY THE

Municipal Gas Light Co.

OFFICE,

No. 952 BROADWAY,

Near 23d Street.

THE Scientific American.

THIRTY-THIRD YEAR.
THE MOST POPULAR SCIENTIFIC PAPER IN THE WORLD.

Only $3.20 a Year, including Postage. Weekly. 52 Numbers a Year. 4,000 book pages.

THE SCIENTIFIC AMERICAN is a large First Class Weekly Newspaper of sixteen pages, printed in the most beautiful style, *profusely illustrated with splendid engravings*, representing the newest Inventions and the most recent Advances in the Arts and Sciences; including Mechanics and Engineering, Steam Engineering, Railway, Mining, Civil, Gas and Hydraulic Engineering, Mill Work, Iron, Steel and Metal Works; Chemistry and Chemical Processes; Electricity, Light, Heat, Sound; Technology, Photography, Printing, New Machinery, New Processes, New Receipes, Improvements pertaining to Textile Industry, Weaving, Dyeing, Coloring, New Industrial Products, Animal, Vegetable, and Mineral. New and Interesting Facts in Agriculture, Horticulture, the Home, Natural History, etc.

The most valuable practical papers, by eminent writers in all departments of Science, will be found in the Scientific American; the whole presented in popular language, free from technical terms, illustrated with engravings, and so arranged as to interest and inform all classes of readers, old and young. The Scientific American is promotive of knowledge and progress in every community where it circulates. It should have a place in every Family, Reading Room, Library, College or School. Terms, $3.20 per year, $1.60 half year, which includes prepayment of postage. Discount to Clubs and Agents. Single copies ten cents. Sold by all Newsdealers. Remit by postal order to MUNN & CO., Publishers, 37 Park Row, New York.

PATENTS. In connection with the Scientific American, Messrs. MUNN & CO. are Solicitors of American and Foreign Patents, and have the largest establishment in the world. Patents are obtained on the best terms. Models of New Inventions and Sketches examined, and advice free. A special notice is made in the Scientific American of all Inventions Patented through this Agency, with the name and residence of the Patentee. Public attention is thus directed to the merits of the new patent, and sales often effected.

Any person who has made a new discovery or invention can ascertain, free of Charge, whether a patent can probably be obtained, by writing to the undersigned. Address for the Paper, or concerning Patents,

MUNN & CO., 37 Park Row, New York.
Branch Office, Cor. F & 7th Sts., Washington, D. C.

Empire Steam Printing Establishment,

13 SPRUCE STREET, NEW YORK.

W. H. GIFFING,

(Successor to TORREY BROTHERS.)

COMMERCIAL

AND

Exhibition Printing

OF EVERY DESCRIPTION.

In a Diversity of Colors and Tints, at a Small Advance over ordinary plain Black Work.

JOB PRINTING

OF ALL KINDS, SUCH AS

Cards, Invitations, Law Cases, Bill Heads, Programmes, Pamphlets, Circulars, Hand-bills, Catalogues.

In the Best Style of the Art, at short notice and reasonable Prices.

LONDON AND MANCHESTER
PLATE GLASS COMPANY,
LIMITED,

WORKS, { SUTTON and RAVENHEAD.   ST. HELENS, LANCASHIRE, ENGLAND.   Address P. O. BOX 4140.

Depot, 94 Maiden Lane,

J. A. WALLER, JR. AGENT.   NEW-YORK,

Manufacturers of the Celebrated

British Polished Plate Glass.
ALSO,
Looking Glass Plates,
POLISHED PLATE

Of Special Thickness from $\frac{1}{8}$ to 1 inch thick.

Chequered and Ground Plate,
Rough and Ribbed Plate,

For FLOORS and SKYLIGHTS, in all thicknesses at lowest market prices.

ESTIMATES FURNISHED ON APPLICATION.

THE PLATE GLASS USED
IN THE TANKS OF THE

New York Aquarium
WAS
MANUFACTURED BY THIS COMPANY.

REASONS WHY

You should Buy the "TEACHER'S BIBLE," issued by the American Tract Society.

OUR SHEETS are printed from the best plates abroad. The Berean Question Book for 1878 adopts the references of our "Large Print" edition, in preference to any other.

OUR HELPS are more complete, and more useful for the teacher than any other issued so far as we know.

OUR MAPS are all new, redrawn within a year, and brought down to the latest authorities.

OUR BINDINGS are unsurpassed by any in the world. We invite critical comparison and examination.

OUR LEVANT BINDINGS are all full flexible, and will open so the sides of the back will touch without injuring them.

OUR PRICES are as low as books honestly made can be sold.

OUR PRICES are uniform, and we do not make a discount to one man and deny it to another, but treat all alike.

OUR BOOKS are commended by such men as Vincent, Trumbull, Sherwin, Gracey, and everybody else that has ever used them.

CIRCULARS AND SPECIMEN PAGES FREE.

AMERICAN TRACT SOCIETY,
150 Nassau St., New York.

A carefully selected stock of fine Singing Canaries, Whistling Bullfinches, Trained Starlings, Fancy Birds of all kinds for the Aviary, Talking Parrots, Pet Animals, Gold Fish, Sea Shells, Aquaria, &c. Also the best and largest assortment of Cages in the city. Seeds and Mocking Bird Food; also Cage Fixtures of all kinds at WILKINS', **1247 Broadway**, between 30th and 31st Streets, New York.

Flowers & Plants.

SIEBRECHT & WADLEY,

Floral Decorators, Nurserymen and Landscape Gardeners,

409 Fifth Avenue cor. 37th St., New York,

NURSERIES AT ASTORIA, L. I.

Send for our **BOOK** Just Published.

A guide for all who love Flowers and Plants. Copies will be sent on application, free of charge.

REMINGTON'S
BREECH-LOADING, DOUBLE-BARRELED GUN.

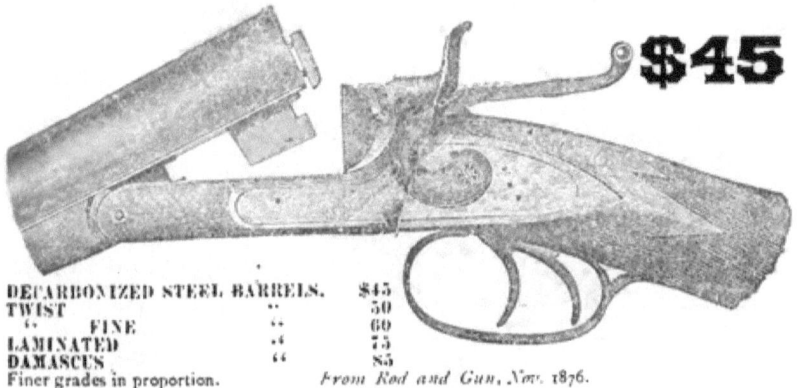

$45

DECARBONIZED STEEL BARRELS.		$45
TWIST	"	50
" FINE	"	60
LAMINATED	"	75
DAMASCUS	"	85

Finer grades in proportion. *From Rod and Gun, Nov. 1876.*

THE REMINGTON GUN.

Judge H. A. Gildersleeve, of the American Rifle Teams, 1874, 1875 and 1876, Lieut. Col. 12th Regt., writes thus under date of Nov. 10th:

"I have just returned from the Big South Bay, where I have been gunning for ducks. I tried for the first time the Remington, 10 gauge gun, I purchased from you last summer. My success with it was excellent. In my judgment its shooting capacity cannot be surpassed. I want no better gun and if I did I don't believe I could find it, even among the expensive grades of English guns.
H. A. GILDERSLEEVE.

Manufactured by E. REMINGTON & SONS, 281 and 283 Broadway, New York. P. O. Box 3991. Armory, Ilion, N. Y. Chicago, 237 State St.; Boston, 146 Tremont St.; St. Louis, 609 North Fourth St.; Baltimore, 47 North Charles St.; Washington, 808 F St. Send for "Illustrated Catalogue and Treatise on Rifle Shooting."

REMINGTON SPORTING RIFLE REDUCED TO $20 AND UPWARDS.

Photo-Electrotyping

Is the name of a new process of engraving by means of photography. It is entirely different from all other methods of photo-engraving—superior to wood engraving in point of depth; and in many instances fully equal to steel and copper plate work. We can reproduce music and small type cheaper than it can be set up. Music publishers can make a great saving in printing by having their lithograph title pages of music reproduced and 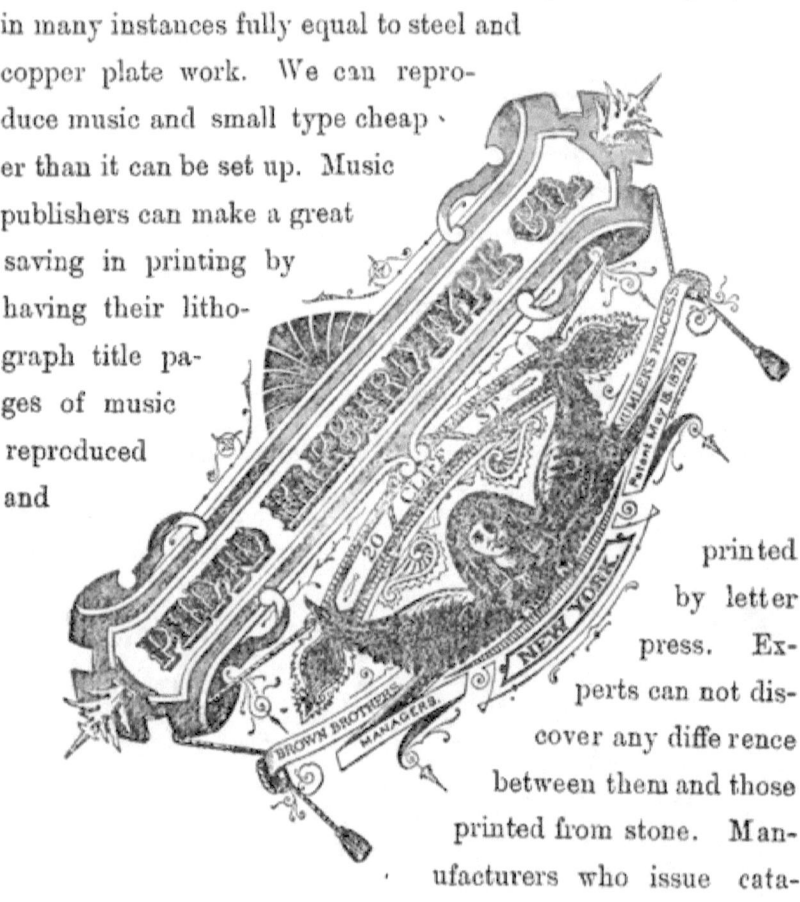 printed by letter press. Experts can not discover any difference between them and those printed from stone. Manufacturers who issue catalogues can also make a great saving, by reducing the size one-half, which can be done at small expense, thereby enabling them to issue a book which is novel in itself, equally as readable, and for one-half the cost.

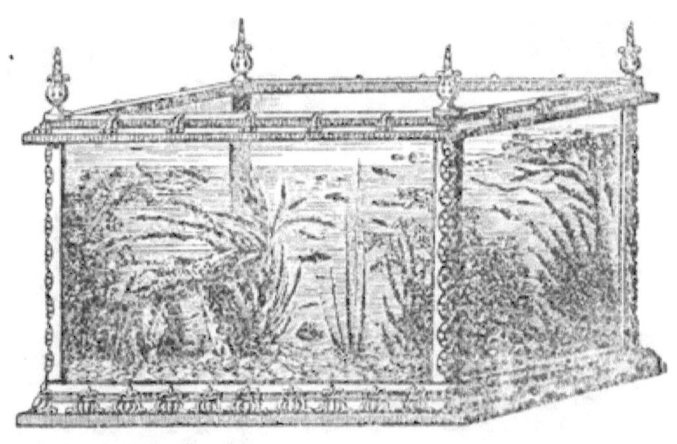

B. GREENWOOD,

Manufacturer of

Aquaria and Aquarium and Greenhouse Cement.

DEALER IN

Fish-Food, Gold Fish, Water-Plants and Aquarium Stock of all descriptions.

Canaries, Cages, Hanging Baskets, Brackets, Sea Shells, Corals, &c.

Also Marine Stock of all kinds, such as Sea Anemones, Serpulae, Crabs, Shrimps, always on hand.

Nos. 11½ to 13 COLLEGE PLACE,

Near Murray Street.   NEW--YORK.

OSBORN MANUFACTURING CO.
79 BLEECKER ST., N. Y.

Bright Metal Bird and Animal Cages.

Illustrated Catalogues and Price List, with Directions for the Care of Birds, sent free on application.

THESE CAGES ARE SOLD BY ALL FIRST CLASS DEALERS.

CAGES REFINISHED AT SHORT NOTICE.

W. H. BROWNING,

BUILDER,

Makes a Specialty in Ornamental and Plain

Cement Work.

DOES ALSO

ALL KINDS OF MASON WORK

In the most substantial manner, giving a guarantee of perfect satisfaction in every case.

THE SPLENDID

Tanks of the New York Aquarium

Were built under his personal superintendence and he refers to the Architect of the Aquarium,

A. B. OGDEN, Esq., and to Messrs. W. C. COUP and CHAS. REICHE & BRO. as to his ability and uprightness as a practical Builder and Contractor.

Office 443 East 77th St.

G. GUNTHER,
Manufacturer of Patented
BRASS, SILVER-PLATED & JAPANNED
BIRD CAGES.
Established 1848.

1876.
Medal & Diploma Awarded to

G. Gunther,

For Good Workmanship, Variety of Patterns, and fitness for purpose intended. (Signed by the Jurors and Centennial Commission.)

103 & 105 WILLIAM ST., N. Y.

EUGENE B. BLACKFORD,

Salmon Factor,

Fish, Lobster, Green Turtle, Soft Crabs & Terrapins,

72, 73, 74, 75, 76, 78, 80, 82, 84 & 86 Fulton Market,.

STOREHOUSES,

134 BEEKMAN & 223 FRONT STREET, NEW YORK.

SPECIALTIES.

Diamond Back Terrapin,   Green Turtle,
Restigouche Salmon,   Brook Trout,
Live Eels,

And all kinds of rare fish constantly on hand at all seasons.

RESTIGOUCHE SALMON.

This is the best flavored Salmon in the world, and I beg leave to inform my numerous patrons that I have contracted to take the entire catch of the estuary fishing on the Restigouche River, and shall receive daily consignments by special Refrigerator cars, by which fresh Salmon will be landed in New York 48 hours after they are taken from the nets. These fish were first put upon the market and introduced to public notice by me during the summer of 1876, and by epicures were pronounced the finest Salmon in the world.

EUGENE G. BLACKFORD,

Received the Highest Award and Medal of Honor for the finest and largest exhibit of Live Fish in tanks, also for the largest and best display of Food Fishes preserved in Patent Refrigerators.

REPORT OF JUDGES:

The undersigned, having examined the product herein described, respectfully recommends the same to the United States Centennial Commission for Award, for the following reasons, viz:

For Collection of Live Fish in Aquaria, and for a very general exhibit of almost all the edible fish found on the Atlantic Coast, with specimens from the Pacific, and from the Rivers and Lakes of the United States. For keen interest taken by Mr. Eugene G. Blackford in American Fishes, and assistance rendered by him in the study of Ichythology.   J. ANDERSON [*Signature of the Judge.*]

APPROVAL OF GROUP JUDGES.

S. F. BAIRD.   T. B. FERGUSON.

A true copy of the record,   { FRANCIS A. WALKER,
                                        Chief of the Bureau of Awards.

Given by authority of the United   { J. L. CAMPBELL, *Secretary*.
     States Centennial Commission.   { A. T. GOSHORN, *Director General.*
                                               { J. R. HAWLEY, *President.*

Messrs. Tiffany & Co.

UNION SQUARE, NEW YORK,

Invite an inspection of their

STOCK OF DIAMONDS

And other Precious Stones,

HOUSEHOLD SILVERWARE,

Artistic Bronzes and Pottery,

FINE STATIONERY,

Watches, General Jewelry,

BRIC-A-BRAC,

Electro Plated Ware

AND

TABLE CUTLERY.

Visitors incur no obligation to purchase.

The Atheneum Publishing House.

D. I. CARSON & CO.,
100 Nassau Street,   New York.

Announcement for 1878.

In addition to our own publications, we propose to continue our Order business; and all Standard Publications, American and Foreign, will be furnished upon short notice, post free, at publishers' prices. We are frequently able to fill orders from job lots or slightly used books, at SPECIAL DISCOUNTS.

Authors and others desiring to publish Books, Monographs or Pamphlets, will find it to their advantage to call.

Atheneum Printing Works.

This department of our business will hereafter be under the special direction of Mr. D. I. CARSON, for several years and until recently General Agent of the Photo-Engraving Company. We are prepared to undertake every variety of PRINTING, ENGRAVING and LITHOGRAPHING, at moderate prices. We employ skilled workmen and can execute the finest work.

Stationery Department.

We are prepared to furnish everything in the line of STATIONERS' GOODS, and make a specialty of WEDDING STATIONERY, VISITING and NOTE CARDS. We also furnish FINE PAPETERIES with Monograms to order in WATER COLORS PUT ON BY HAND, something new and elegant. We are also sole Eastern Agents for BROWN'S "PERFECT" LETTER FILE, the best in use.

Address Orders and Inquiries to,

D. I. CARSON & CO.,
100 NASSAU STREET

CHAS. REICHE & BRO.,

Importers,

55 CHATHAM STREET, N. Y.,

And Alfeld, Hanover, Germany.

RARE BIRDS AND ANIMALS,

Singing Birds, and Birds of Beautiful Plumage.

FOREIGN ANIMALS OF EVERY KIND FROM ALL PARTS OF THE WORLD.

Prepared Food.   *Cages.*

Orders received to procure any kind of living bird or animal.

GOODS SHIPPED TO ALL PARTS.

www.ingramcontent.com/pod-product-compliance
Lightning Source LLC
Chambersburg PA
CBHW021919180426
43199CB00032B/931